The Definitive Guide to Masonite

Building Web Applications with Python

Christopher Pitt
Joe Mancuso

Apress®

The Definitive Guide to Masonite: Building Web Applications with Python

Christopher Pitt
Cape Town, South Africa

Joe Mancuso
Holbrook, NY, USA

ISBN-13 (pbk): 978-1-4842-5601-5
https://doi.org/10.1007/978-1-4842-5602-2

ISBN-13 (electronic): 978-1-4842-5602-2

Managing Director, Apress Media LLC: Welmoed Spahr
Acquisitions Editor: Steve Anglin
Development Editor: Matthew Moodie
Coordinating Editor: Mark Powers

Cover designed by eStudioCalamar

Cover image designed by Raw Pixel (www.rawpixel.com)

Distributed to the book trade worldwide by Apress Media, LLC, 1 New York Plaza, New York, NY 10004, U.S.A. Phone 1-800-SPRINGER, fax (201) 348-4505, e-mail orders-ny@springer-sbm.com, or visit www.springeronline.com. Apress Media, LLC is a California LLC and the sole member (owner) is Springer Science + Business Media Finance Inc (SSBM Finance Inc). SSBM Finance Inc is a **Delaware** corporation.

For information on translations, please e-mail editorial@apress.com; for reprint, paperback, or audio rights, please email bookpermissions@springernature.com.

Apress titles may be purchased in bulk for academic, corporate, or promotional use. eBook versions and licenses are also available for most titles. For more information, reference our Print and eBook Bulk Sales web page at http://www.apress.com/bulk-sales.

Any source code or other supplementary material referenced by the author in this book is available to readers on GitHub via the book's product page, located at www.apress.com/9781484256015. For more detailed information, please visit http://www.apress.com/source-code.

Printed on acid-free paper

Table of Contents

About the Authors

Christopher Pitt is a developer and writer, working at Indiefin. He usually works on application architecture, though sometimes you'll find him building compilers or robots. He is also the author of several web development books and is a contributor on various open source projects such as AdonisJs and Masonite.

Joseph Mancuso is the creator, maintainer, and BDFL for Masonite. He has been a software developer for over a decade and the CEO of Masonite X Inc, a company based around all things Masonite related. He's an avid contributor of open source, a consultant for Masonite-adopted companies, and freelance worker for companies using Masonite.

About the Technical Reviewers

 **Alfredo Aguirre** is a senior software engineer who helps a wide range of online companies such as Mozilla, Google, R/GA, Elsewhen, and Stink Studios to transform their ideas into digital products while ensuring they perform and scale to meet the business requirements. He is based in London, UK, and can be contacted at `https://madewithbytes.com/`.

Vaibhav Mule has been programming in Python for 5 years at various organizations. He started off as an early adopter for the Masonite framework and is actively involved in maintaining Masonite and Masonite ORM.

You can learn more about him at `vaibhavmule.com`.

CHAPTER 1

Getting Started

By writing this book, we hope to teach you how to build great applications, using the Masonite framework (`https://github.com/masoniteframework/masonite`). Masonite is a modern Python framework, which includes tools and conventions aimed at making that task easier.

It's ok if you're new to Python. It's ok if you're new to Masonite. The book is written so that you can still get the most out of it. There may be some more advanced topics, along the way, but we'll do our best to make them additional and not essential to your experience.

If you've never used Python, we recommend this short course to get you familiar with the basics: `https://teamtreehouse.com/library/python-basics-3`.

The things you'll need are a computer on which to install Python, some time to read, and some time to experiment. It doesn't need to be a fancy computer, and it doesn't need to be a huge amount of time.

We've arranged the chapters so that you can learn about core concepts of the framework and build toward a functional application. You can read this book as a reference guide. You can read it as a series of tutorials. You can read it one chapter at a time, or altogether.

Thank you for taking the first step toward becoming a Masonite pro.

"Where Do I Begin?"

There are many different kinds of programming. The one you're probably most familiar with is application programming, which is where you install an application (or use an installed application) on a phone, tablet, or computer.

Come to think of it, you're also probably familiar with another kind: web site programming. These kinds of programs are used through a web browser like Chrome, Safari, or Firefox.

© Christopher Pitt and Joe Mancuso 2020
C. Pitt and J. Mancuso, *The Definitive Guide to Masonite*, https://doi.org/10.1007/978-1-4842-5602-2_1

Masonite sits somewhere in the middle of these two kinds of programs. Let me explain why.

Python was originally designed as a system programming language. That means it was intended to be used in short server administration scripts, to configure other software and to perform batch operations.

Over time it has become a powerful, multi-paradigm programming language. Some programming languages are mainly used for web programming, and they are used through web servers, like Apache and Nginx. Other languages take more complete control over how a web server behaves. Python is one of the latter languages.

Python web applications, and Masonite applications in particular, are usually responsible for everything from listening on a port to interpreting an HTTP request to sending an HTTP response. If something's wrong with a Masonite application, something's wrong with the whole server. With this increase in risk comes an increase in flexibility.

In addition, controlling the whole server gives us the ability to do more advanced things, like serving web sockets and interacting with external devices (like printers and assembly lines).

How Masonite Handles Releases

Before we look at code, it's important to talk about how Masonite handles releases. Big frameworks, like Masonite, change quickly. You may start a project on version 2.1, but in a few weeks version 2.2 is released. This can lead to some important questions:

- Should I upgrade?

- What does an upgrade entail?

- How often does this happen?

Let's answer these, one at a time.

Should I Upgrade?

Upgrades are a good thing, but sometimes they have trade-offs.

Functionality may be deprecated, meaning it is flagged for future removal. There may be multiple changes you need to make, so that your application will work in the new version. You may uncover bugs or things you've not tested for.

Having said all that, upgrades can also bring new features and security fixes. The security benefits alone are reason enough to take any upgrade seriously.

The best thing to do is review the upgrade guide and decide whether the cost of the upgrade is worth the benefits it brings. There's no harm in staying a few major versions back, so long as you're still using a minor version of the framework that can receive security updates (and so long as there are no obvious security issues with the version you're using).

You can find an up-to-date upgrade guide on the documentation web site: `https://docs.masoniteproject.com/upgrade-guide`.

What Does an Upgrade Entail?

This question is easily answered by reading through the upgrade guide. If you're a few versions behind, you may need to go through multiple upgrade guides to get fully up-to- date.

Masonite uses a three-part version scheme: `PARADIGM.MAJOR.MINOR`.

This means you should have little-to-no issues when upgrading from `2.1.1` to `2.1.2`. Upgrades from `2.1` to `2.2` are a bit more involved, but I've found they generally take 10 minutes or less, assuming I've not veered too far from the conventions of the framework.

In contrast to this versioning scheme, each Masonite library uses Semantic Versioning (`https://semver.org`). If you're using individual Masonite libraries, as opposed to the whole framework, then you're pretty safe upgrading from `2.1` to `2.2` without breaking changes.

How Often Does This Happen?

Masonite follows a 6-month release cycle. This means you can expect a new `MAJOR` version every 6 months. These releases aim to require less than 30 minutes to upgrade.

If they're expected to take more than that, they're shifted into a new `PARADIGM` version.

Installing the Dependencies

Masonite needs a few dependencies to work well. While we're installing those, we may also talk a bit about how best to write Python code. To begin with, let's install Python.

Installing Python and MySQL on macOS

I work on a Mac, so that's where I'd like to start things off. macOS doesn't come with a command-line package manager (like what you'd expect in Linux), so we'll need to install one.

For this section, we're going to assume you have a recent version of macOS installed, with access to the Internet.

Open Safari, and go to https://brew.sh. This is the home of Homebrew. It's a great package manager, which will provide us with ways to install Python 3 and a database.

There's a command, front and center. It should look something like

```
/usr/bin/ruby -e "$(curl -fsSL https://raw.githubusercontent.com/Homebrew/
install/master/install)"
```

It says to download a Ruby script from that URL, executing it with the Ruby interpreter most macOS systems have installed. If you're feeling particularly suspicious, feel free to open that URL in Safari and inspect its contents.

It's good to be suspicious of sites that tell you to blindly execute scripts from the Internet. In this case, Homebrew has a reputation for security and utility. They're balancing ease of installation against the potential for that suspicion.

If you still consider this too risky, check toward the end of this section, where I recommend a more in-depth resource for setting up new Python environments.

Running this command, in terminal, will begin the process of installing Homebrew. It takes a bit of time and will ask questions along the way. One of those questions is whether you would like to install the Xcode command-line tools.

You don't really have a choice, if you want to be able to use Homebrew. Those utilities include compilers for the code Homebrew downloads, so it won't be able to install much without them.

When the installation is complete, you should be able to start installing dependencies through Homebrew. The ones we're interested in are Python 3 and MySQL 5.7. Let's install them:

```
$ brew install python3
$ brew install mysql@5.7
```

After installing MySQL, you'll be given some instructions for starting the server. I recommend you follow these, or you won't be able to log in or make changes to the database.

You can verify the version of Python and MySQL by running

```
$ python --version
$ mysql --version
```

You should see Python 3.x.x and mysql ... 5.7.x installed.

If that command tells you that you're still using Python 2.x, then you may need to add the path, suggested at the end of the python3 installation, to your PATH variable. Mine looked something like this:

```
export PATH="/usr/local/opt/python/libexec/bin:$PATH"
```

This is from ~/.zshrc, but you should put it in ~/.profile or ~/.bashrc, depending on how your system is set up.

Run the --version commands, in a new terminal window, and you should see Python 3.x.x as the version.

Installing Python and MySQL on Linux

Next up, we're going to look at how to install these dependencies on Debian/Ubuntu Linux. Here, we have access to a command-line package manager, called aptitude.

You can use the following commands to install Python and MySQL:

```
$ sudo apt update
$ sudo apt install python-dev libssl-dev
$ sudo apt install mysql-server-5.7
```

If the `apt` command isn't present, you're probably using a slightly older version of Linux, where you should use `apt-get` instead.

It's a good idea to start the MySQL server, or you won't be able to log in or make changes to it:

```
$ systemctl start mysql
$ systemctl enable mysql
```

You can verify the version of Python and MySQL by running

```
$ python --version
$ mysql --version
```

You should see `Python 3.x.x` and `mysql ... 5.7.x` installed.

Editing Code

You should use the code editor, or integrated development environment, that you're most comfortable with. We recommend you use something like Visual Studio Code, as it contains just enough automated tooling to be useful, but is still fast and free.

You can download it at `https://code.visualstudio.com`.

As you open Masonite files, you'll see prompts to install Code extensions. These will give you handy tips and tell you when you have an error in your code. We recommend you install these when prompted.

Setting Up in Other Environments

If you're using macOS or Linux, these instructions should be fine for you. If you're using a different version of Linux, or Windows, you will probably need to follow a different guide for installing Python on your system.

A good place to look is the official Masonite documentation: `https://docs.masoniteproject.com`.

If you're looking for a refresher of the Python language, check out `www.apress.com/la/book/9781484200292`.

Creating a New Masonite Application

One of the tools Masonite provides, to help with project creation and maintenance, is a global command-line utility. Along with Python, the preceding instructions should also have installed a dependency management tool called Pip. We can install Masonite's command-line utility, using Pip:

```
pip install --user masonite-cli
```

Depending on how your system is set up, you may have to use a binary called `pip3` instead. If you're unsure which to use, run `which pip` and `which pip3`. These will give you hints as to where the binaries are installed, and you can pick whichever binary looks better to you.

After this command has finished executing, you should have access to Masonite's command-line utility, `craft`. You can verify this by inspecting its version:

```
craft --version
```

Now, it's time to create a new Masonite project. Navigate to where you'd like the project's code folder to reside, and run the new command:

```
craft new friday-server
```

You can substitute your own project name where you see `friday-server`. I've called mine that, for reasons that will become obvious in a bit.

You should then be prompted to navigate into the newly created folder and run an `install` command. Let's do that:

```
cd friday-server
craft install
```

This command installs the dependencies Masonite needs to run. After running this code, you should see some text telling you "key added to your .env file".

To make sure everything is working, let's run the `serve` command:

```
craft serve
```

This should tell you that the application is being served at "`http://127.0.0.1:8000`", or something similar. Open that URL in your browser, and you should be greeted with the Masonite 2.1 landing page as shown in Figure 1-1.

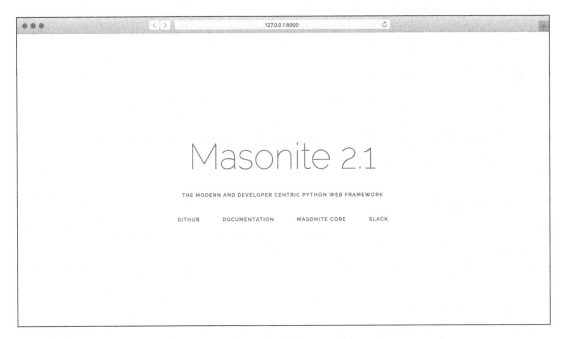

Figure 1-1. *The Masonite 2.1 landing page*

Exploring the Masonite Folder Structure

We're going to be spending a lot of time in this codebase, so a basic understanding of the folder structure (as shown in Figure 1-2) will be beneficial to us knowing where to create new files and change existing ones.

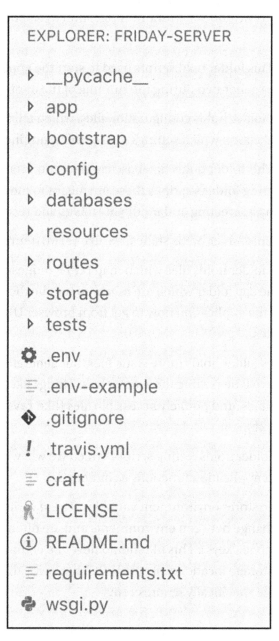

Figure 1-2. *The Masonite 2.1 folder structure*

Let's look at what each of these files and folders are for, without going into too much detail:

1. app – This folder starts off holding the parts of the application that respond to individual HTTP requests and apply blanket rules and restrictions to all requests and responses. We'll be adding lots to this folder, as we add ways for the application to respond to requests.

2. bootstrap – This folder hold scripts used to start the application and cache files generated during the running of the application.

3. config – This folder holds configuration files, which tell the Masonite application which settings to use while running.

4. databases – This folder holds database configuration scripts. Unlike the config folder's scripts, these are meant to modify an existing database, creating and modifying tables and records.

5. resources – This folder holds static files, like HTML templates.

6. routes – This folder holds files which map HTTP requests to the parts of the app folder which are meant to handle them. It's where we tell the application how to get from browser URLs to application files.

7. storage – This folder holds more static files, but generally they're the kind that we'll be putting there ourselves. Things like file uploads, Sass files, and publicly accessible files (like favicon.ico and robots.txt).

8. tests – This folder holds testing scripts, which we will write to make sure our application functions as intended.

9. .env – This file stores environment variables. These variables are likely to change between environments and are often secret values (like service keys). This file should never be committed to shared code storage locations, like GitHub. That's why the default .gitignore file specifically ignores .env.

There are other files which are generally found in Python applications. When appropriate, we'll talk about these files.

As we build our example application, we'll start to add files and change these existing files. When you see paths to files, you can assume that we're talking about them as relative to the base folder.

Planning the Example Application

Some people find it easier to learn a tool when they're using that tool to build something. For that reason, in this book, we're going to build an example application.

It's not essential that you follow along with the example, since the main focus of the book is the theoretical and technical usage of Masonite libraries. It's merely additional to what you'll learn about Masonite, as a means of solidifying your learning.

I love experimenting with electronics, and this excitement has only grown after seeing movies like *Iron Man*. In *Iron Man* the viewer gets to know a man named Tony Stark, who has built mansions full of tech to automate every aspect of his life.

After watching those movies, I had a strong urge to do the same.

When we were planning this book, we were trying to think of interesting topics for an example project, and this idea came to mind. So, we're going to build our example project with the goal of automating parts of our lives.

We'll begin with simple tasks, like implementing podcast and media center management, and continue on to larger things like getting up-to-date weather reports and automatically responding to emails.

If we have time, we'll even delve into the world of electronics, connecting devices to our code and having them perform physical tasks for us.

Following the trend of the movies, I want to call my home automation and personal assistant persona Friday. I am beyond excited at the potential of this example application, and I hope you find it as stimulating to your learning as we intend for it to be.

Summary

In this chapter, we took the first steps toward learning about Masonite. We installed some tools and created a new application. We're going to build on this application through the rest of the book.

We also discussed the theme of this example application. As we continue, feel free to add your own design and flair to the example. It's meant to keep you interested in using Masonite, and hopefully becomes something useful to you by the end of the book.

CHAPTER 2

Routing

In the previous chapter, we set things up to be able to start building a Masonite application. We installed Python, a database, and the craft command-line utility.

In this chapter, we're going to learn about the process of connecting browser URLs to the application code that handles each request. We'll learn about the different types of requests Masonite can interpret, and we'll start to build functionality for our example application.

"How Does Masonite Handle Requests?"

The Internet is built around the idea of request/response cycles. The same few things happen, whenever you open a browser and enter a URL:

1. Your browser connects the address you type in (like `www.apress.com`) with an IP address. IP addresses come in two forms: IPv4 and IPv6. Both of these are types of addresses that are meant to connect different machines together, but are not easy for humans to deal with.

    Things called Domain Name Servers (or DNS for short) have lookup tables which take in the human-readable domain names and give out the IPv4 or IPv6 address back to the browser.

2. The browser makes a request to the server, at the end of the IPv4 or IPv6 address (and usually at port 80 or port 443). After DNS resolution, a request to `www.apress.com` will result in the browser sending a request to `151.101.172.250:443` (the address might be different when you try it, since servers can change their IP addresses).

3. The server then has a chance to interpret the request and respond accordingly. Most of the time, the response will be a textual body (which can contain HTML) and some headers describing the server and response body.

© Christopher Pitt and Joe Mancuso 2020
C. Pitt and J. Mancuso, *The Definitive Guide to Masonite*, https://doi.org/10.1007/978-1-4842-5602-2_2

It's the third step where Masonite takes over. Masonite applications listen on port 80 and port 443, unless otherwise configured, and are given the HTTP request to interpret.

HTTP means Hypertext Transfer Protocol, and it describes the format in which requests are made and responses are sent. There's a huge amount of detail I'm glossing over, because it's largely unimportant to what we're learning about Masonite. If you'd like to see the full specification, you can find it at `https://tools.ietf.org/html/rfc2616`.

Masonite takes in an HTTP request, performs some initial formatting on it, and passes that request to a route handler. In order for us to respond to specific requests, we need to create route handlers and the accompanying controllers.

Creating Controllers and Routes

This code can be found at `https://github.com/assertchris/friday-server/tree/chapter-2`.

In Masonite, we think of routes as the first point of entry into the application, but before we can create new routes, we have to create new controllers.

The craft command has built-in functionality to help us create new controllers with little effort. Inside our project folder, we can use the following command:

```
craft controller Home
```

This will create a file, called `HomeController.py`, in the `app/http/controllers` folder. Controllers are the glue between HTTP requests and responses. The one we just made looks like this:

```
"""A HomeController Module."""

from masonite.request import Request
from masonite.view import View

class HomeController:
    """HomeController Controller Class."""
```

```
def __init__ (self, request: Request):
    """HomeController Initializer

    Arguments:
        request {masonite.request.Request}...
    """
    self.request = request
    def show(self, view: View):
        pass
```

This is from app/http/controllers/HomeController.py.

Controllers are ordinary Python classes. What makes them powerful is that they are created and called using a dependency injection container. We'll dive deeply into what that means, in Chapter 3.

For now, all you need to know is that the Request and View objects you see, there, will automatically be provided. We don't need to create new instances of this controller, and feed it with those objects, in order for it to function.

Most of the controller code is documentation. For the sake of brevity, we're going to omit as much of this kind of documentation as possible. You'll see it in your files (and it'll still be in ours), but we won't be repeating it in code listings.

Now that we've made a controller, we can connect it to a route. If you open routes/web.py, you'll notice it already has a defined route. You've probably also noticed the existing controller. Forget about those, for a minute. Let's add our own route, to respond to GET requests at /home:

```
from masonite.routes import Get, Post

ROUTES = [
    # ...
    Get().route('/home', 'HomeController@show').name('home'),
]
```

This is from `routes/web.py`.

This should be enough, right? Let's start the server up:

```
craft serve
```

Older versions of Masonite require a -r flag to make the server restart every time it sees a file change. If your updates aren't showing in the browser, make sure the server is reloading every time a file changes, by checking in the console. If you're not seeing any activity, there, you may need this flag.

When we open the server in a browser (at `http://127.0.0.1:8000/home`), we see the screen shown in Figure 2-1.

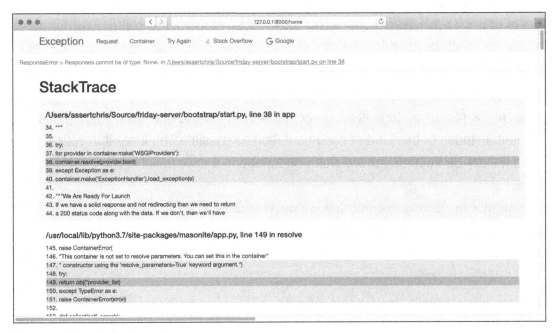

Figure 2-1. *Oops! An error*

That can't be normal, can it? Well, let's go back to the controller code:

```
from masonite.request import Request
from masonite.view import View

class HomeController:
    def __init__ (self, request: Request):
        self.request = request

    def show(self, view: View):
        pass
```

This is from app/http/controllers/HomeController.py.

Our route tells Masonite to use the show method, but the show method just passes. For routes to work, they need to return something. The error message tells us this, albeit in a roundabout way: "Responses cannot be of type: None."

The fix is surprisingly simple. We just need to return something form the show method. A plain string will do:

```
def show(self, view: View):
    return 'hello world'
```

This is from app/http/controllers/HomeController.py.

Figure 2-2. *Returning a string from* show

Success! This may not seem like much, but it's the first step toward building a functional application.

Let's review what has happened so far:

1. We opened a browser to http://127.0.0.1:8000/home. The browser created an HTTP request and sent it to that address.

2. The Masonite server, started with craft serve -r and listening on port 80, received the HTTP request.

3. The Masonite server looked for a route matching /home, with the GET request method. It found a match and looked at which controller and method to use.

4. The Masonite server fetched the prevailing Request and View objects, instantiated the controller, and sent those objects to the controller and show methods.

5. We told the controller to return a string, for that type of request, which it did. That string was formatted as an HTTP response and sent back to the browser.

6. The browser displayed the HTTP response.

Every route you create will be connected with a method in a controller, or directly to a response file. You'll need to follow this process often, so it's important that you get the hang of it now.

This is just an ordinary GET route, but there are many different kinds of routes and variations we can use.

Creating Different Kinds of Routes

We've kinda glossed over this, but HTTP requests can have different aspects that separate them. We've already seen what GET requests look like – the kind that happen when you type and address into your browser.

Different Methods

There are a few other methods:

- POST – These kinds of requests usually happen when you submit a form in your browser. They are used to signify that the object(s) being conveyed on should be created on the server.

- PATCH, PUT – These kinds of requests usually don't happen in the browser, but they have special meaning and operate similarly to POST requests. They are used to signify that the object(s) being conveyed on should be partially changed or overwritten, respectively.

- DELETE – These kinds of requests also don't usually happen in the browser, but they operate similarly to GET requests. They are used to signify that the object(s) being conveyed should be removed from the server.

- HEAD – These kinds of requests do happen in the browser, but they are more about the metadata of the object(s) being conveyed than they are about the object(s) themselves. HEAD requests are ways to inspect the object(s) in question and whether the browser has permission to operate on them.

Using these request methods, requests to the same path (like /room) can mean different things. A GET request can mean that the browser, or person using it, wants to see information about a specific room.

A POST, PATCH, or PUT request may indicate that the user wants to make or change a room, specifying attributes to create or change it with.

A DELETE request may indicate the user wants the room removed from the system.

Different Parameters

Routes (and requests) can also have different kinds of parameters. The first, and easiest to think about, is the kind of parameter that is part of the URL.

You know when you see blog posts, with URLs like https://assertchris.io/post/2019-02-11-making-a-development-app..? That last part of the URL is a parameter, which could be hard coded or could be dynamic, depending on the application.

We can define these kinds of parameters by changing how the route looks:

```
from masonite.routes import Get, Post

ROUTES = [
    # ...
    Get().route('/home/@name', 'HomeController@show')
    .name('home'),
]
```

This is from routes/web.py.

Notice how we've added /@name to the route? This means we can use URLs like /home/ chris, and that chris will be mapped to @id. We can access these parameters in the controller:

```
def __init__ (self, request: Request):
    self.request = request

def show(self, view: View):
    return 'hello ' + self.request.param('name')
```

This is from app/http/controllers/HomeController.py.

The __init__ method (or the constructor) accepts a Request object, which we can access inside the show method. We can call the param method, to get the named URL parameter, which we defined in the route.

Since we only have the show method, and all __init__ is doing is storing the Request object, we can shorten this code:

```
from masonite.request import Request
from masonite.view import View

class HomeController:
    def show(self, view: View, request: Request):
        return 'hello ' + request.param('name')
```

This is from app/http/controllers/HomeController.py.

This works, as before, because controller methods are called after their dependencies have been resolved from the dependency injection container.

If you're using a dependency in a single method, you should probably just accept that parameter in the same method. If you're reusing it multiple times, it's a bit quicker to accept the dependency in the constructor.

Another way to parameterize a request is to allow query string parameters. This is when a URL is requested, but ends in syntax resembling ?name=chris. Let's make the @name part of the route optional and allow for it to be given as a query string parameter instead:

```
from masonite.routes import Get, Post

ROUTES = [
    # ...
    Get().route('/home/@name', 'HomeController@show')
    .name('home-with-name'), Get().route('/home', 'HomeController@show')
    .name('home-without-name'),
]
```

This is from `routes/web.py`.

The quickest and easiest way to make a parameter optional is to define a second route that doesn't require it to be provided. Then, we have to modify the controller to work with both:

```python
from masonite.request import Request
from masonite.view import View

class HomeController:
    def show(self, view: View, request: Request):
        return 'hello ' + (
            request.param('name') or request.input('name')
        )
```

This is from `app/http/controllers/HomeController.py`.

We can access query string parameters using the `input` method, on the `Request` object. Wanna know the best part about this code? If we want to respond to POST, PATCH, or PUT requests, we don't need to change any of this controller code.

We can modify the `/home` routes to accept GET and POST requests:

```python
from masonite.routes import Get, Post, Match

ROUTES = [
    # ...
    Match(['GET', 'POST'], '/home/@name',
          'HomeController@show').name('home-with-name'),
    Match(['GET', 'POST'], '/home',
          'HomeController@show').name('home-without-name'),
]
```

This is from `routes/web.py`.

We have to allow insecure POST requests to these URLs, in the CSRF middleware:

```python
from masonite.middleware import CsrfMiddleware as Middleware

class CsrfMiddleware(Middleware):
    exempt = [
        '/home',
        '/home/@name',
    ]

    every_request = False
    token_length = 30
```

This is from app/http/middlware/CsrfMiddleware.py.

We're going to be learning about middleware in Chapter 8 and CSRF protection in Chapter 4. For now, it's enough to know that POST requests are usually prevented when they come from outside the application.

Browser requests should continue to work, but now we can also make POST requests to these endpoints. The easiest way to test this is to install an app called Postman. Here are the steps for testing:

1. Go to www.getpostman.com and download and install the app. You'll need to create a free account when you open the app, unless you've used Postman before.

2. Change the method dropdown from Get to Post and enter the URL httsp:// 127.0.0.1:8000/home.

3. Change the data tab from Params to Body and enter name (key) = chris (value).

4. Click Send.

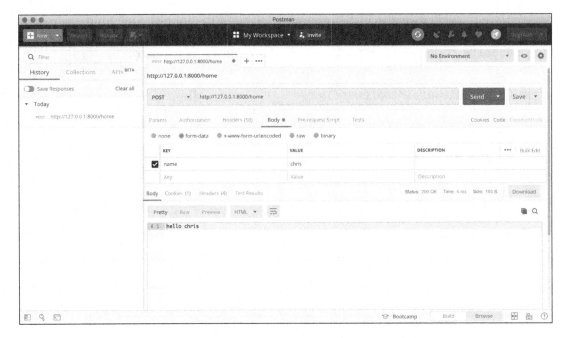

Figure 2-3. *Sending POST requests to the server*

If either the GET or POST request gives you an error, along the lines of "can only concatenate str (not "bool") to str," it's probably because you're providing neither the route *param* nor the query string/post body name.

Route Groups

Sometimes you want to configure multiple routes to be similarly named, or to behave in similar ways. We can simplify the /home routes by grouping them together:

```
from masonite.routes import Get, Match, RouteGroup


ROUTES = [
    # ...
    RouteGroup(
        [
            Match(['GET', 'POST'], '/@name',
                'HomeController@show').name('with-name'),
            Match(['GET', 'POST'], '/',
```

```
            'HomeController@show').name('without-name'),
    ],
    prefix='/home',
    name='home-',
  )
]
```

This is from `routes/web.py`.

If we use `RouteGroup` instead of `Match` or `Get`, we can define common path and name prefixes. This saves a lot of typing and makes it easier to see routes that have something in common.

There are a few more advanced aspects of `RouteGroup`, but they are best left for the chapters where they are properly explained. Look out for middleware in Chapter 8 and domains (deploying) in Chapter 13.

Exploring Request and Response

While we're in the controller, let's look at the Request and Response classes in a bit more detail. We've already used a couple Request methods, but there are more to see.

We've seen how to request a single named input, but there's also a way to get all input for a request:

```
request.all()
```

This returns a dictionary of input. For `HEAD`, `GET`, and `DELETE` methods, this probably means query string values. For `POST`, `PATCH`, and `PUT` methods, this probably means request body data.

The latter methods can send their body data as URL-encoded values, or even as JSON data.

I say this "probably means" because the latter methods may also have query string values. While this is allowed in most settings, it's contrary to the HTTP specification. When you're designing your application to use the latter methods, you should try to steer clear of mixing query strings and body data.

`request.all()` is useful, in situations where you're unsure exactly what data you're expecting. There are variations of this method, which get a bit more specific:

```
request.only('name')
request.without('surname')
```

These methods limit the returned dictionary items and exclude the specified dictionary items, respectively.

If you're not sure what input you're expecting, but you want to know of certain keys are present, then there's another method you can use:

```
request.has('name')
```

`request.has()` returns True or False, depending on whether or not the specified key is defined. You could, for instance, alter the behavior of the route method, based on the presence of certain bits of data. Perhaps you want to update a user's account details, if you detect data specific to that. Or, perhaps you need to reset their password, if you find relevant data in their form submission. Up to you.

Reading and Writing Cookies

One of the ways we remember a user, and store data relevant to their session, is by setting cookies. These can be set and read in the browser, so it's important to realize that the Masonite defaults protect against this.

Cookies can be set, using this method:

```
request.cookie('accepts-cookies', 'yes')
```

We won't be able to read this, using JavaScript, unless we also disable HTTP-only and server-side encryption:

```
request.cookie(
    'accepts-cookies',
```

```
    'yes',
    encrypt=False,
    http_only=False,
    expires='5 minutes',
)
```

This code also demonstrates how to set the expiry of cookies. By default, they will expire the moment the user closes their browser, so any long-lived or persistent data must have this value set.

Cookies can be read in a couple ways. The first is by specifying a key:

```
request.get_cookie('accepts-cookies', decrypt = False)
```

If you set Encrypt to False, then you need to set Decrypt to False. Otherwise the Decrypt argument may be omitted. If Masonite tries to decrypt a cookie, but fails, then it will delete that cookie. This is a security precaution against cookie tampering.

If you want to manually delete a cookie, you can do so with this method:

```
request.delete_cookie('accepts-cookies')
```

Sending Other Kinds of Responses

So far, we've only sent plain strings back to the browser. There are a myriad of other responses we could be sending, beginning with JSON responses:

```
return response.json({'name': 'chris'})
```

This kind of response will have the appropriate content type and length headers appended to the response. We can make it even shorter, by returning a dictionary:

```
return {'name': 'chris'}
```

It's this kind of magic that makes me enjoy Masonite so! There's something similar happening when we return plain strings, but this is the first time we're digging deep enough to know that is what's happening.

Now, imagine we wanted to redirect the user, instead of returning some renderable response to the browser. We can use the redirect method for that:

```
return response.redirect('/home/joe')
```

This isn't too flexible on its own. We can, however, use a similarly named Request method, to redirect to a named route:

```
return request.redirect_to(
    'home-with-name',
    {'name': 'chris'},
)
```

This is one of the main reasons I recommend you always name your routes. If you later want to change the path to the route, all the code that references a named route will continue to function unmodified. It's also often quicker using a named route than it is reconstructing or hard coding the URL you need.

Creating Views

The final kind of response I want to talk about is the kind that involves HTML. If we're interested in building a rich UI, plain strings just aren't going to cut it. We need a way to construct more complex templates, so we can show dynamic and styled interface elements.

Let's see what it would look like if we make the /home routes show dynamic HTML. The first step is to create a layout file:

```
<!doctype html>
<html lang="en">
    <head>
        <meta charset="utf-8">
    </head>
    <body>
        @block content
            <!-- template content will be put here-->
        @endblock
    </body>
</html>
```

This is from `resources/templates/layout.html`.

It's a good idea to build our templates to fit inside a layout, so that global changes can be applied in one place. We'll see this come into play, shortly. For now, let's create a home template:

```
@extends 'layout.html'

@block content
    <h1>hello {{ name }}</h1>
@endblock
```

This is from `resources/templates/home.html`.

Notice how little this template has to repeat, since we're extending the `layout.html` template. This path is relative to the templates folder. Blocks defined in "outer" templates can be overridden by "inner" templates. This means we can define default content, which "inner" templates can replace with more specific content.

> Masonite views use a superset of the Jinja2 template syntax, which can be found at `http://jinja.pocoo.org/docs`. One important difference is that Masonite templates can use `@extends` syntax in place of `{%extends ...%}` syntax.

There are a couple things we need to change, in the controller, to use these templates. Firstly, we're using dynamic data, in the form of `{{ name }}`. This data needs to be passed into the view. Secondly, we need to specify which view template to load.

Here's how that code looks:

```
def show(self, view: View, request: Request):
    return view.render('home', {
        'name': request.param('name') or request.input('name')
    })
```

This is from `app/http/controllers/HomeController.py`.

We pass the name data, to the view, by defining a dictionary of dynamic data.

There's a lot more to learn about the Jinja2 syntax and how Masonite extends it. We'll explore it more as we build our example application.

Starting the Example Application

Before we begin, I want to stress that the example application is entirely optional to your learning. Each chapter's example code can be found on GitHub, so you don't have to retype anything.

That said, we highly recommend that you at least follow along with the development of the example application. We believe you'll find it easier to remember what you learn if you see it built into something real. More so if you build something real yourself.

This code can be found at `https://github.com/assertchris/friday-server/tree/between-chapters-2-and-3`.

I listen to many podcasts, so I'd like Friday (my personal assistant and home automation software) to organize and play podcasts on demand. Friday will begin her life as a glorified podcast app.

Let's start by creating a page through which to search for new podcasts. We need a new controller and template:

```
craft controller Podcast
craft view podcasts/search
```

This new controller is exactly the same as the HomeController we created, except in name. We should rename the show method, so it more accurately reflects what we want to show:

```
from masonite.view import View

class PodcastController:
    def show_search(self, view: View):
        return view.render('podcasts.search')
```

This is from app/http/controllers/PodcastController.py.

This new view is just an empty file, but it's in the right location. Let's give it some markup, so we can tell whether or not it's being correctly rendered:

```
@extends 'layout.html'

@block content
    <h1>Podcast search</h1>
@endblock
```

This is from resources/templates/podcasts/search.html.

Before this will work, we need to add a route. We can start with a RouteGroup, because we expect to add more routes, with similar names and prefixes.

```
from masonite.routes import Get, Match, RouteGroup

ROUTES = [
    # ...
    RouteGroup(
        [
            Get().route('/', 'PodcastController@show_search')
            .name('-show-search')
        ],
        prefix='/podcasts',
        name='podcasts',
    ),
]
```

This is from routes/web.py.

If you're running the `craft serve -r` command, you only need to go to /podcasts in the browser to see this new page. It looks a bit ugly, so I think we should start applying some styles. Let's use a tool called Tailwind (`https://tailwindcss.com`), since it's easy to get started with:

```
npm init -y
npm install tailwindcss --save-dev
```

This adds two new files and one new folder. You can commit the files to Git, but I recommend adding the folder (which is node_modules) to your .gitignore file. You can always recreate it by running npm install.

Masonite provides an easy way to build Sass (`https://sass-lang.com`) for our application. We can add the following link to our layout file:

```
<!doctype html>
<html lang="en">
    <head>
        <meta charset="utf-8">
        <link href="/static/style.css" rel="stylesheet" type="text/css">
    </head>
    <body>
        @block content
            <!-- template content will be put here-->
        @endblock
    </body>
</html>
```

This is from `resources/templates/layout.html`.

This /static/style.css file doesn't exist, but that's because it is being redirected to storage/compiled/style.css. This file is generated from what we put into storage/static/sass/style.css. We can add new styles, to that file, and see them reflected in our application:

```scss
@import "node_modules/tailwindcss/dist/base";
@import "node_modules/tailwindcss/dist/components";
@import "node_modules/tailwindcss/dist/utilities";

h1 {
    @extend .text-xl;
    @extend .font-normal;
    @extend .text-red-500;
}

input {
    @extend .outline-none;
    @extend .focus\:shadow-md;
    @extend .px-2;
    @extend .py-1;
    @extend .border-b-2;
    @extend .border-red-500;
    @extend .bg-transparent;

    &[type="button"], &[type="submit"] {
        @extend .bg-red-500;
        @extend .text-white;
    }
}
```

This is from `storage/static/sass/style.scss`.

This will only work if we've installed the Sass library, using `pip install libsass` or `pip3 install libsass`. You may, also, not see changes just by refreshing the page. If you aren't seeing changes, restart the server and clear your browser cache.

I don't want to go into too much detail about Tailwind, except to say that it is a utility-based CSS framework. That means styles are applied by giving elements classes (inline), or extracting classes in the way we've done with these h1 and input selectors.

Let's also reposition the content so that it sits in the middle of the page:

33

```
<!doctype html>
<html lang="en">
    <head>
        <meta charset="utf-8">
        <link href="/static/style.css" rel="stylesheet" type="text/css">
    </head>
    <body>
        <div class="container mx-auto py-4">
            @block content
                <!-- template content will be put here-->
            @endblock
        </div>
    </body>
</html>
```

This is from `resources/templates/layout.html`.

Let's also add a search form and some dummy results:

```
@extends 'layout.html'

@block content
    <h1 class="pb-2">Podcast search</h1>
    <form class="pb-2">
        <label for="terms" class="hidden">Terms:</label>
        <input type="search" name="terms" id="terms" />
        <input type="submit" value="search" />
    </form>
    <div class="flex flex-row flex-wrap">
        <div class="w-full md:w-2/5 mr-2 flex flex-row pb-2">
            <div class="min-h-full w-48 bg-red-300"></div>
            <div class="p-4 flex flex-col flex-grow">
                <div class="mb-8 flex flex-col flex-grow">
                    <div class="text-xl mb-2">Title</div>
                    <p class="text-base">Description</p>
                </div>
```

```
        <div class="flex flex-grow items-center">
            <div class="w-10 h-10 bg-red-300"></div>
            <div class="text-sm ml-4">
                <p class="leading-none">Author</p>
                <p class="">date</p>
            </div>
        </div>
    </div>
</div>
<div class="w-full md:w-2/5 mr-2 flex flex-row pb-2">
    <div class="min-h-full w-48 bg-red-300"></div>
    <div class="p-4 flex flex-col flex-grow">
        <div class="mb-8 flex flex-col flex-grow">
            <div class="text-xl mb-2">Title</div>
            <p class="text-base">Description</p>
    </div>
    <div class="flex flex-grow items-center">
        <div class="w-10 h-10 bg-red-300"></div>
        <div class="text-sm ml-4">
            <p class="leading-none">Author</p>
            <p class="">date</p>
        </div>
    </div>
    </div>
</div>
</div>
<div class="w-full md:w-2/5 mr-2 flex flex-row pb-2">
    <div class="min-h-full w-48 bg-red-300"></div>
    <div class="p-4 flex flex-col flex-grow">
        <div class="mb-8 flex flex-col flex-grow">
            <div class="text-xl mb-2">Title</div>
                <p class="text-base">Description</p>
            </div>
            <div class="flex flex-grow items-center">
                <div class="w-10 h-10 bg-red-300"></div>
                <div class="text-sm ml-4">
```

```
                    <p class="leading-none">Author</p>
                    <p class="">date</p>
                </div>
            </div>
        </div>
    </div>
</div>
@endblock
```

This is from `resources/templates/podcasts/search.html`.

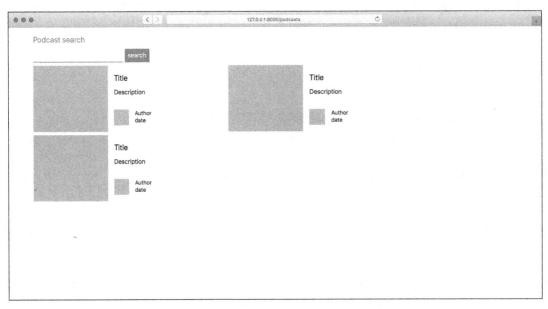

Figure 2-4. *Podcast search form and results*

Summary

In this chapter, we learned about controllers, routing, and views. We created multiple entry points into our application, accepted multiple request methods, and responded with simple and complex responses.

We also began work on our personal assistant application, got Sass up and running, and started applying styles to custom markup.

In the next chapter, we're going to learn about some of the more advanced tools Masonite provides, beginning with the dependency injection container.

CHAPTER 3

The Service Container

Masonite is built around what is called a "service container." Don't let this wording confuse you though. All a service container is just a group of... services, exactly! Services in this context are just features. Think of the service container as a toolbox, services as your tools, and Masonite as your workshop. A service can be as small as a `Mail` class for sending mail or a `Queue` class for sending jobs to a message broker like RabbitMQ. Services can even get more advanced like a routing engine to map the URL to a given controller.

All of these services are loaded (bound) into the service container, and then we fetch the service at a later time. More on why this is important later on.

The real benefit of a service container is that it handles application dependencies for you. Take the example of all the time you had to:

- Import an object.

- Initialize the object.

- Pass some data to a setter method.

- Finally call the object methods.

- Do the same thing in several files.

Masonite's service container is also called an IoC container. Service container and IoC container will be used interchangeably. IoC stands for Inversion of Control. Inversion of Control simply means that the conventional control of objects is flipped. When normally an object is responsible for

- Finding the object

- Instantiating the object

with Masonite's IoC container, all objects are

- Instantiated

- Handed to the object

© Christopher Pitt and Joe Mancuso 2020
C. Pitt and J. Mancuso, *The Definitive Guide to Masonite*, https://doi.org/10.1007/978-1-4842-5602-2_3

See how the control has inverted? The benefit of building an application that is wrapped around a service container is actually really simple. There are two major benefits the container has.

The first benefit is that it allows you to load all of your services (objects) into the container at the beginning of when your application boots up (like starting the server) which is then used throughout your entire application. This removes the need to have to instantiate a class in multiple places. It also allows you to swap that class out with any other class at a later time. Maybe you don't like the logging class you are using so you swap it out for another implementation.

The second benefit is that it allows you to link most of your classes together that depend on each other. For example, if a Logger class needs the Request and Mail class, Masonite will wire them all together and give you the completed and initialized class ready to use. There is no need to wire all your application dependencies together. This saves a lot of time is invaluable to a maintainable codebase.

Let's get started on a bit more about the container.

The Problem We Are Solving

Take this as an example. We have two very simple classes.

The first class sends a simple email from the request object and logs a message saying that the email is sent:

```
from some.package import SMTPMail, BaseMail

class Mail(BaseMail):
    def __init__ (self, request, logger):
        self.request = request
        self.logger = logger

    def send(self, message):
        self.to(self.request.input('email')).smtp(message)
```

Simple enough, right? We may use this inside a controller method like this:

```
from masonite.request import Request
```

```
from app.mail import Mail
from app.logger import Logger

class MailController:

    def show(self, request: Request):
        logger = Logger(level='warning', dir='/logs')
        mail = Mail(request, logger)
        mail.send('Email has been sent!')
```

This code may look fine, but notice how we had to set up a new object called logger just to pass that information to the mail class. Imagine for a second that we had to use this class in ten different files. Maybe 20 other objects had to use this Logger class. Are we really going to import it every time into the file, initialize it, and pass it in?

Type Hinting

Now notice we have a line in the preceding method signature that looked like this:

```
def show(self, request: Request):
```

This is called "type hinting" and it is the basis for how we will primarily be interacting with the service container.

Type hinting is the art of telling a parameter which type it should be. We may tell a parameter to be a Request class or a Logger class.

On the Masonite side, Masonite will say "oh this parameter wants to become a Logger class. I already know about that logger class so I will force that parameter to be the same object I already know about."

A type hint is semantically written like this:

```
from some.package import Logger

def function(logger: Logger):
  pass
```

The syntax is {variable}: Class.

The variable can be named whatever you like. For example, the signature can be written any of these ways:

```
def function(log:  Logger):

def function(logging: Logger):

def function(l: Logger):
```

The variable is simply just that, a variable. Name it whatever you like.

There are several places throughout the codebase where Masonite will inspect objects before calling them. These places are things like controllers, middleware, and queue job methods. These are just places that Masonite resolves for you, but you can always resolve your own classes as well.

Service Providers

Now you may be wondering how the heck does Masonite know which class to provide? I asked for the Logger class and I got the Logger class. So how does Masonite know which class to provide?

This is all done by what Masonite calls "service providers."

Service providers are simple classes that are used to inject services into the container. They are the building blocks that make up a Masonite application. Masonite checks its service provider list and uses that to bootstrap the application. Masonite is actually made up primarily of these service providers.

This is an example of a service provider list:

```
from masonite.providers import AppProvider, SessionProvider, ...

PROVIDERS = [
    # Framework Providers
    AppProvider,
    SessionProvider,
    RouteProvider,
    StatusCodeProvider,
    WhitenoiseProvider,
    ViewProvider, HelpersProvider,
]
```

This is the simple flow of the core of a Masonite application:

1. WSGI server (like Gunicorn) first starts up.

2. Masonite runs through the list of service providers and runs the `register` method on all of them.

3. Masonite runs back through and runs all the `boot` methods on all service providers where `wsgi = False`. This `wsgi = False` attribute just tells Masonite that we don't need a WSGI server to be running to bootstrap this portion of the application. If `wsgi = True`, then Masonite will run the `boot` method on every single request. If we have a service provider that loads a `Mail` service in the container, it does not need to be run on every request.

4. Masonite will then listen on a specific port for any requests.

5. When a request hits the server (like the homepage), then the Masonite will run the `boot` method on only the service providers where `wsgi = True` or the attribute does not exist (it's `True` by default). These are providers that need to be run like mapping a request URL to a route and controller or loading the WSGI environment into the request object.

You can tell by the preceding bullet points that Masonite is entirely dependent on this service container. If you need to swap out the functionality of Masonite, then you swap out the service container.

In the flow of things, you will build out classes that perform a specific service (like logging) and then use a service provider to put it into any Masonite application.

A simple service provider will look like this:

```
from masonite.providers import ServiceProvider

class SomeServiceProvider(ServiceProvider):

def register(self):
    pass

def boot(self):
    pass
```

The Register Method

Let's break down the service provider a bit more because if you know how this works, then you are on your way to writing extremely maintainable code within your Masonite application.

The register method is first to run on all service providers and is the best place to bind your classes into the container (more on binding in a bit). You should never try to fetch anything from the container inside the register method. This should be reserved only for putting classes and objects in.

We can register classes and objects by using the bind method. Binding is the concept of putting an object into the container.

```
from some.package import Logger

..

def register(self):
    self.app.bind('Logger', Logger(level='warning', dir='/logs'))
```

We also want Masonite to manage the application dependencies for our new Mail class:

```
from some.package import Logger, Mail

..

def register(self):
    self.app.bind('Logger', Logger(level='warning', dir='/logs'))
    self.app.bind('Mail',  Mail)
```

The classes have now been put into the container. Now we can do what's called "type hinting" it into our mail class.

```
from some.package import Logger

class Mail:

    def __init__ (self, logger: Logger):
      self.logger   =   logger
```

Now when Masonite attempts to construct this class, it will go to initialize the class but say "hey I see you want a Logger class. Well, I have that logger class already. Let me give you the one I know about which is already set up inside my container."

Now when we resolve this Mail class, it will act something like this:

```
from some.place import Mail

mail = container.resolve(Mail)
mail.logger #== <some.package.Logger x82092jsa>
```

We'll talk more about resolving in a bit, so don't let this part confuse you yet. Now notice the Logger class Masonite knew about was passed into the Mail class for us because we type hinted it.

The Boot Method

The boot method is where you will do most of your interaction with the container. Here is where you will do things like construct classes, tweak classes already in the container, and specify container hooks.

A typical service provider that adds mail functionality will look like this:

```
from some.place import MailSmtpDriver, Mail

class MailProvider(ServiceProvider):

    wsgi = False

    def register(self):
        self.app.bind('MailSmtpDriver',  MailSmtpDriver)
        self.app.bind('Mail', Mail)

    def boot(self, mail: Mail):
        self.app.bind('Mail', mail.driver('smtp'))
```

So what we did here was we bound a MailSmtpDriver as well as the full Mail class into the container when it is registered. Then after all providers are registered, we resolved the Mail class back out of the container and then bound it back into the container but with the driver set as smtp.

This is because there could be other service providers that register additional mail drivers into the container so we want to interact with the container only after everything has been registered.

The WSGI Attribute

You will notice that there is a wsgi attribute that is either set to True or False. Showing only the first half of the class, it looks like this:

```
class MailProvider(ServiceProvider):

    wsgi = False

    def register(self):
```

If this attribute is either missing or set to True (it is True by default), then it will run on every single request. But we see here that we are only adding a new mail feature, so we really don't need it to run on every request.

Nearly all service providers will not need to run on every request. Service providers that need to run on every request are primarily those vital to the framework itself like the "RouteProvider" which takes the incoming request and maps it to the correct route.

Something important as well on these providers you may see is a "wsgi = True" parameter. This property will be used to indicate that specific providers should run on every request. If you need to run code based on a CSRF token of the user, that could change between requests, so you will need to set the attribute to True. You should find that most application level service providers simply need to bind more classes into the service container so this attribute is usually set to False.

Another provider that runs on every request is the StatusCodeProvider which will take a bad request (e.g., 404 or 500) and show a generic view during production.

But now that we have a provider that simply binds a few classes to the container and we don't need anything related to the request, we can make sure that wsgi is False.

The only downside to not doing this is that it will just take some extra time on the request to execute code that really doesn't need to execute.

More on Binding

There are some important things to note when it comes to the bind method. There are basically two types of objects we can bind into the container which are classes and initialized objects. So let's go through what these two types of objects are.

Class vs. Object Behavior

Classes are simple uninitialized objects, so looking back to our previous Mail class, we have this example:

```
from some.place import Mail

mail = Mail # this is a class
mail = Mail() # this is an uninitialized object
```

This is important because you can have several different objects. If you modify one object, it does not modify the other object. Take this as an example:

```
from some.place import Mail

mail1 = Mail()
mail2 = Mail()

mail1.to = 'user@email.com'
mail2.to #== '' empty
mail2.to = 'admin@email.com'
```

So because of this behavior, we can bind a class into the container and not an initialized object:

```
from some.place import Mail

container.bind('Mail', Mail)
```

Now every time we resolve it, it will be different because it is constructed each time:

```
from some.place import Mail

container.bind('Mail', Mail)
```

```
mail1 = container.resolve(Mail)
mail2 = container.resolve(Mail)

mail1.to = 'user@email.com'
mail2.to #== '' empty
mail2.to = 'admin@email.com'
```

Now that we know this behavior, we can also bind initialized objects into the container. **This will be the same object no matter how many times we resolve it.** See this example now:

```
from some.place import Mail

container.bind('Mail', Mail())

mail1 = container.resolve(Mail)
mail2 = container.resolve(Mail)

mail1.to = 'user@email.com'
mail2.to #== 'user@email.com'
```

Binding classes this way is useful because you can add new service providers which can manipulate your objects for you. So adding a service provider may add a full session-based feature to your request class. Since it's the same object, any interaction with the initialized class in the container will have the same functionality when we resolve it back out later.

The downside, or upside depending on your use case, is that doing it this way requires you to manually set up your classes since we need to construct the full object before we bind it into the container.

So going back to our Logger and Mail example, we would have to do something like this:

```
from some.place import Mail, Logger

container.bind('Mail', Mail(Logger()))

mail1 = container.resolve(Mail)
mail2 = container.resolve(Mail)

mail1.to = 'user@email.com'
mail2.to #== 'user@email.com'
```

Not too big of a deal, but this is just a simple example.

In this case, we will call for the singleton pattern.

Binding Singletons

A singleton is a very simple concept. It just means that anytime we need this class, we want the same exact class every time. Masonite achieves this simply by resolving the class **when we bind it**. So the instantiated object goes into the container, and it will always be that exact same object throughout the lifetime of the server.

We can bind singletons into the container by doing

```
from some.package import Logger, Mail

..

def register(self):
  self.app.bind('Logger', Logger)
  self.app.singleton('Mail', Mail)
```

Then whenever we resolve it, we will get the same object every time as well as the Logger object. We can prove this by fetching it and checking the memory location:

```
mail1 = container.make('Mail')
id(mail1) #== 163527
id(mail1.logger)  #==  123456

mail2 = container.make('Mail')
id(mail2) #== 163527
id(mail2.logger) #== 098765
```

Notice the Mail classes are the same, but the Logger classes are different.

Simple Binding

We have noticed that sometimes we are duplicating ourselves when we bind into the container. Most of our binding keys are just the name of our classes. In order to get around this, we can use the simple binding.

```
# Instead of:
def register(self):
  container.bind('Mail', Mail)

# We can do:
def register(self):
  container.simple(Mail)
```

These two lines of code are exactly the same, and we can now make it as we normally would use the class name as the key:

```
container.make('Mail')
```

Resolving Classes

So we have touched on briefly how to resolve an object with objects already in the container, but let's talk more about what resolving actually does.

Resolving simply means we will take the objects parameter list, extract what objects are type hinted, find them in our container, and then inject them into the parameter list and return the new object.

It's important to note that an object we are resolving does not need to be in the container, **but all of the parameters do.** So if we are resolving the Mail class we have been working with, we don't need to bind the Mail class into the container, but the Logger class inside the Mail class initializer does. If it is not, then Masonite will throw an exception since it cannot correctly build the object.

So a code example would look like this:

```
from some.place import Mail, Logger

container.bind('Logger', Logger)

mail = container.resolve(Mail)
mail.logger #== <some.place.Logger  x098765>
```

Notice the Mail class is not in the container but its dependencies are. So we can correctly build this object for you.

Hooks

Hooks are another interesting concept. Hooks are useful when you want to intercept the resolving, making, or binding of an object.

We can register callables with hooks by using one of three methods to register our callable: on_make, on_bind, on_resolve.

On Make

An example would be something like this:

```
def change_name(obj):
  obj.name = 'John'
  return  obj
...

def register(self):
  self.app.on_make('Mail',  change_name)

def boot(self):
  mail = self.app.make('Mail')
  mail.name #== 'John'
```

Notice that it fired this hook when we used the make method. This is because the make method fires the on_make hook and looks for any registered hooks and passes the object into it before returning it.

On Bind

Following the previous example, we can do the same thing when we bind the object into the container:

```
def change_name(obj):
  obj.name = 'John'
  return  obj
...

def register(self):
  self.app.on_bind('Mail', change_name)
```

```
mail = self.app.make('Mail')
mail.name #== 'John'
```

Notice it is doing the same thing as in the preceding example, but on the back end, the hook is run when we bind the object.

On Resolve

The last hook is done every time we resolve the object:

```
from some.place import Mail, TerminalLogger

def change_logger(obj):
  obj.logger = TerminalLogger()
  return obj
...

def register(self):
  self.app.bind('Mail', Mail)
  mail = self.app.make('Mail')
  mail.logger #== <some.place.Logger x098765>

def boot(self, mail: Mail):
  mail.logger #== '<some.place.TerminalLogger    x098765>'
```

Notice when we used the bind and make methods, our hook was never run. Not until we resolved it was the logger changed. This is doubly useful for testing when you want to modify some attributes on a class before it hits your test cases.

Swapping

Another awesome feature of the service container is the ability to swap out classes for other classes. This is useful when you want to simplify your type hinting or want to code to abstractions rather than concretions.

Here is a code snippet example:

```
from some.place import ComplexLogger, TerminalLogger, LogAdapter
```

```
container.swap(
  TerminalLogger,
  ComplexLogger(LogAdapater).driver('terminal')
)
```

Now, whenever we resolve this TerminalLogger class, we will instead get back whatever the more complex logger is:

```
from some.place import TerminalLogger

def get_logger(logger: TerminalLogger)
    return logger

logger = container.resolve(get_logger)
logger #== '<some.place.ComplexLogger x098765>'
```

This is very good when it comes to building to abstractions rather than concrete classes. We can swap out complex implementations with more complex ones in a nice simple way.

Design Pattern Knowledge

In order to become an absolute expert on the service container, I think it is important to grasp some knowledge first before continuing. This should give you enough well-rounded knowledge to fully grasp everything. You might even need to reread this chapter a few times to make everything click better if you are still unsure about anything.

Coding to Abstractions

A common design pattern in software design is the concept of dependency inversion. Dependency inversion is a definition. All it means, in very simple terms, is that you want to rely on an abstract class and not have to worry about the direct class itself. This is useful when you need to change the lower-level classes out for something different down the road.

For example, if you are using a `TerminalLogger`, then you actually want to never use the `TerminalLogger` class itself but instead want to use some abstraction of it like a new `LoggerConnection` class. This class is called an abstract class because the `LoggerConnection` could be anything. It could be a terminal logger, a Sentry logger, a file logger, etc. It's abstract because the class `LoggerConnection` is not actually clear what it is using and therefore its implementation can be swapped out at any time later.

Dependency Injection

We have talked already about dependency injection and you might not have even realized it. This is another 10*phrase fora*1 definition. All dependency injection is doing is passing in a dependency into an object.

This can be as simple as passing in a variable to a function like this:

```
def take(dependency):
    return dependency

inject_this = 1
x = take(inject_this)
```

That's it! We have just done dependency injection. We took a dependency (the "*inject_this*" variable) and gave it to (or injected it into) the `take` function.

Inversion of Control (IoC)

Ok, so this is the simple one. This is the same as the preceding dependency injection, but it just depends on **where** the logic is happening. If the dependency injection is coming from you, it's just normal dependency injection, but if it is coming from the container or framework, it is Inversion of Control.

This is why Masonite's service container is sometimes referenced as an IoC container.

This is any new information but just background knowledge that will allow you to better understand what exactly the container is trying to achieve.

Implementing Abstractions

Setting Up Our Abstraction

Let's start by making our LoggerConnection class. We can code to abstractions by making a simple base class which our concrete classes will inherit from:

```
class LoggerConnecton:
  pass
```

Then we can build our terminal logger and inherit from our new LoggerConnection class:

```
from some.place import LoggerConnection

class TerminalLogger(LoggerConnection):

  def log(self, message):
    print(message)
```

Now the last step is to bind the TerminalLogger into our container. We'll do this in our register method of one of our service providers:

```
from some.place import TerminalLogger

class LoggerServiceProvider:

  def register(self):
    self.app.bind('Logger', TerminalLogger)
```

Great! Now we are all set up to code to an abstraction. Remember our abstraction was the LoggerConnection class, so now if we type hint that class, we will actually get our TerminalLogger:

```
from some.place import LoggerConnection

class SomeController:

  def show(self, logger: LoggerConnection):
    logger #== <some.place.TerminalLogger x09876>
```

So you may be wondering how it did this. How this works is that when Masonite is trying to find the `LoggerConnection` class, it keeps track of any class that is a subclass of `LoggerConnection`. Masonite will know that it does not have the `LoggerConnection` in its container and will return the first instance of it instead. In this case, it is the `TerminalLogger`.

Swapping Out Loggers

The biggest benefit of coding this way is that in the future you can switch out the logger for a different logger and never touch any other part of the application. This is how you build a maintainable codebase.

Take this for example. We want to now swap out our `TerminalLogger` for a new and improved `FileLogger`.

First, we construct the class:

```
from some.place import LoggerConnection

class FileLogger(LoggerConnection):

  def log(self, message):
    # Write to log file
    with open('logs/log.log', 'a') as fp:
      fp.write(message)
```

And then we bind it to the container again but remove the previous binding:

```
from some.place import FileLogger

class LoggerServiceProvider:

  def register(self):
    # self.app.bind('Logger', TerminalLogger)
    self.app.bind('Logger', FileLogger)
```

And that's it! Now when we resolve it, we get the `FileLogger`:

```
from some.place import LoggerConnection
```

```
class SomeController:

  def show(self, logger: LoggerConnection):
    logger #== <some.place.FileLogger x09876>
```

We didn't change any other part of our application besides the container binding, and it changed the type of logger everywhere else in the codebase.

Remembering

As you can tell, the resolve method needs to do a lot of things. It needs to inspect the object to see what it is, it needs to extract out the parameter list, it needs to then inspect each parameter one by one, it needs to loop through all the objects in the container, actually find the correct one, and then build the list and inject it into the object for you.

As you can imagine, this is extremely expensive. Not only is it expensive, but it also needs to sometimes run dozens of times per request.

Luckily though, Masonite's container will remember what each object needs to be resolved and caches them. Next time that object needs its dependencies again, like on the next request, it will grab it from a special dictionary it builds and inject them for you.

This can lead to close to at least a 10x boost to your application. Testing shows that resolving a class can go from 55ns per resolve down to 3.2ns per resolve when Masonite remembers object signatures.

Collecting

Collecting is a really awesome feature where you can specify the objects you want from the container, and it will return you a new dictionary of all the objects.

You can collect in two different ways: by key and by the object.

Collecting by Key

You can collect by the key by specifying a wildcard either before, during or after a key name.

Take this, for example, if you want to get all keys that end with Command:

```
container.bind('Request', Request())
container.bind('MigrateCommand', MigrateCommand)
```

```
container.collect('*Command')
#== {'MigrateCommand':  MigrateCommand}
```

Notice we got all objects in the container bound the key via a wildcard of *Command. This will get everything that ends with Command.

You can also work the other way and get everything that starts with a specific key:

```
container.bind('Request', Request())
container.bind('MigrateCommand', MigrateCommand)

container.collect('Migrate*')
#== {'MigrateCommand': MigrateCommand}
```

Notice these are the same since before we were getting everything that started with the Command key and now we are getting everything that starts with the Migrate key. You can also specify the wildcard in the middle of a key:

```
container.bind('Request', Request())
container.bind('SessionCookieDriver', SessionCookieDriver)

container.collect('Session*Driver')
#== {'SessionCookieDriver': SessionCookieDriver}
```

Collecting Session*Driver will get keys like SessionCookieDriver, SessionMemoryDriver or SessionRedisDriver.

This is really useful when you want to bind with a specific format, so you can easily retrieve them again later.

Collecting Objects

You can also collect objects and subclasses of objects. Maybe you have a base class and want to collect all instances of that base class. Masonite uses this for its scheduled tasks package where all tasks inherit a base Task class and we can then collect all the tasks in the container:

```
class Task1(BaseTask):
  pass

class Task2(BaseTask):
  pass
```

```
container.simple(Task1)
container.simple(Task2)

container.collect(BaseTask)
#== {'Task1': Task1, 'Task2', Task2}
```

This is extremely useful if you want to bind objects into the container and then fetch them back out using a parent class. If you are developing a package, then this is a very useful feature.

Application

Ok, so now that you are an expert on the service container, let's look into how we can use all of our knowledge we have gained so far to add an RSS feed to our Friday app. We will:

- Add an RSS feed class into our container

- Add code to abstractions and not concretions

- Resolve the class from the container and use it with our controller method

The Package

A great package to use for this is the feedparser package. So with our application and inside our virtual environment, let's install this package:

```
$ pip install feedparser
```

Let that install and now we'll start building our abstraction class and our concretion class.

Abstraction Class

Our abstraction class will be very simple. It's basically going to be a base class which our concrete class will inherit from.

Let's call this class an RSSParser class. Inside this class, we'll make a parse method which will return the parsed RSS feed we will define on our concrete class.

Let's also create this class manually inside an app/helpers/RSSParser.py class:

```
# app/helpers/RSSParser.py

class RSSParser:

  def parse(self, url):
      pass
```

We called this RSSParser because we will be swapping this implementation with our other RSS parsers in the future, so we needed to give it an abstract enough name where we can do that.

Concrete Class

Since we are using the feedparser library, let's call the concrete class the FeedRSSParser class:

```
# app/helpers/FeedRSSParser.py

import feedparser
from .RSSParser import RSSParser

class FeedRSSParser(RSSParser):

  def parse(self, url):
      return feedparser.parse(url)
```

If that second import in the preceding code is confusing, it just means import the file starting at the current directory. Since both files are in the app/helpers directory, we can import it like this.

The Service Provider

Let's create a new service provider which will be only responsible for handling our RSS feed classes.

We'll want to call it the RSSProvider since it provides RSS classes to our application. We can use craft for this:

```
$ craft provider RSSProvider
```

Once we do that, we can start binding our classes to the container like this:

```
from masonite.provider import ServiceProvider
from app.helpers.FeedRSSParser import FeedRSSParser

class RSSProvider(ServiceProvider):

  wsgi = False

  def register(self):
    self.app.bind('FeedRSSParser', FeedRSSParser())

  def boot(self):
      """Boots services required by the container """

      pass
```

And lastly we need to tell Masonite about our provider, so let's import it into config/providers.py and add it to our list at the bottom:

We will import our provider at the top first and add it near the bottom of the list next to the # Application Providers comment:

```
from app.providers.RSSProvider import RSSProvider
...

    CsrfProvider,
    HelpersProvider,

    # Third Party Providers

    # Application Providers
    RSSProvider,
]
```

The Controller

Ok, now for the final act, we need to use this new abstraction in our controller method.

Creating the Controller

Let's first start by creating a controller we will specifically use for parsing RSS feeds called the FeedController.

The craft command will postfix controller with Controller, so we just need to run this:

```
craft controller Feed
```

Setting Up the Controller

Now here is the part that is very simple, but it could get a bit tricky the first time you did it. Instead of importing and using the concrete class we created earlier, we will import the abstract class we created first.

This means that instead of importing and using FeedRSSParser, we will be importing and using the RSSParser abstract class we created instead.

So let us import this class and return it in our controllers show method now. We'll use an iTunes podcast RSS feed for now at https://rss.itunes.apple.com/api/v1/us/podcasts/top-podcasts/all/10/explicit.rss. Here is an example of the full controller:

```
from app.helpers.RSSParser import RSSParser

class FeedController:
    """FeedController Controller Class."""

    def __init__ (self, request: Request):
        self.request = request

    def show(self, parser: RSSParser):
        return
parser.parse('https://rss.itunes.apple.com/api/v1/us/podcasts/top-podcasts/
all/10/explicit.rss')
```

Refresher on Abstractions and Concretions

Remember about abstractions vs. concretions and how the container can match them up. This is an important concept to grasp. **You do not need to do it this way, but coding to an abstract class instead of a concrete class is typically a good design pattern to follow**. It will make code much more maintainable for 2 or 3 years down the road when one library is abandoned or you need to change to a better or faster library.

In the cases of switching the implementation, you only have to switch out the binding in the service provider and you are done.

The Route

The last step is to set up the route so we can hit this controller method. This is a very simple step that we have gone over already.

```
Get().route('/feed', 'FeedController@show').name('feeds'),
```

Great! Now when we go to the /feed route, we will see the iTunes podcast feed as you can see in Figure 3-1.

```
▼ {
  ▼ "feed": {
      "title": "Top Audio Podcasts",
    ▼ "title_detail": {
        "type": "text/plain",
        "language": null,
        "base": "https://rss.itunes.apple.com/api/v1/us/podcasts/top-podcasts/all/10/explicit.rss",
        "value": "Top Audio Podcasts"
      },
    ▼ "links": [
      ▼ {
          "rel": "alternate",
          "type": "text/html",
          "href": "https://rss.itunes.apple.com/api/v1/us/podcasts/top-podcasts/all/10/explicit.rss"
        },
      ▼ {
          "rel": "self",
          "type": "application/rss+xml",
          "href": "https://rss.itunes.apple.com/api/v1/us/podcasts/top-podcasts/all/10/explicit.rss"
        },
      ▼ {
          "rel": "alternate",
          "type": "text/html",
          "href": "https://itunes.apple.com/WebObjects/MZStore.woa/wa/viewTop?genreId=26&popId=28"
```

Figure 3-1. *The RSS feed response*

CHAPTER 4

Accepting Data with Forms

In previous chapters, we learned a bit about some of the patterns Masonite uses to organize an application. We learned about binding and resolving from the container. We also saw how managers, drivers, and factories are used to create a highly customizable system.

In this chapter, we're going to dive back into the practical aspects of building an application, using these new techniques and tools.

"How Do I Store Data?"

There are many ways to send data, to a web application, using a browser. There are the obvious ways, such as when we enter a web site address into the browser's address bar. We're telling the browser where we want to go, and that request ends up at the web application's doorstep.

In Chapter 2, we saw the many ways in which we can make requests to a Masonite application. What I'm more interested in, for the purposes of this chapter, are some of the other ways we can send and receive data.

Have you heard the term "Ajax" before? It's a name that began as an acronym for a particular set of technologies (**A**synchronous **J**avaScript **A**nd **X**ML), but has become a term to describe many kinds of partial page loading.

In essence, Ajax is when the GET or POST requests we usually send happen quietly behind the scenes, usually to persist some state or reload part of the page with new content.

Then there's web sockets. These are an evolution of the HTTP requests we've seen thus far. Instead of full or partial requests for new content, web sockets are a continuous open connection, through which the server can push new content to the browser.

63

© Christopher Pitt and Joe Mancuso 2020
C. Pitt and J. Mancuso, *The Definitive Guide to Masonite*, https://doi.org/10.1007/978-1-4842-5602-2_4

There are more ways, but these help to illustrate a problem I want us to solve. When we're building web applications, we need to be able to send data along these channels. We also need to validate that the data is in order, before doing something with it. Typically, form data is stored, but it could also be sent to other services, which will expect certain things in certain formats.

So, in this chapter, we're going to work out how to create forms and how to post their data securely to the server. We'll explore the options we have for ensuring the data is properly formatted and doesn't try to do malicious things on the server.

Building Secure Forms

This code can be found at `https://github.com/assertchris/friday-server/tree/chapter-5`.

Let's pick up where we left off, at the end of Chapter 2. We'd built a couple pages, including one to list search results for podcasts, as shown in Figure 4-1.

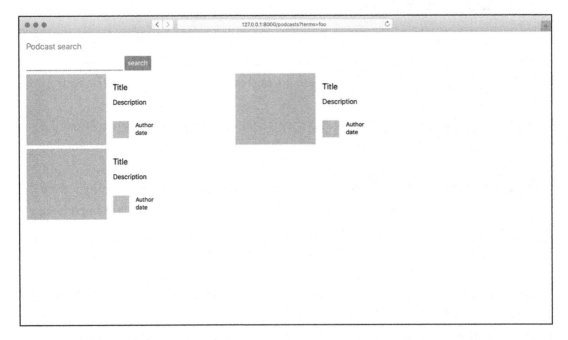

Figure 4-1. *What we have, so far*

We'll begin by making this page dynamic. The first time someone gets to it, we can show an empty search result. We do this by sending an empty list of podcasts to the template and using what's called a conditional:

```python
from masonite.controllers import Controller
from masonite.view import View

class PodcastController(Controller):
    def show_search(self, view: View):
        return view.render('podcasts.search', {
            'podcasts': self.get_podcasts()
        })
    def get_podcasts(self, query="):
        return []
```

This is from app/http/controllers/PodcastController.py.

```
@extends 'layout.html'

@block content
        <h1 class="pb-2">Podcast search</h1>
        <form class="pb-2" method="POST">
                {{ csrf_field }}
                <label for="terms" class="hidden">Terms:</label>
                <input type="search" name="terms" id="terms" />
                <input type="submit" value="search" />
        </form>
        <div class="flex flex-row flex-wrap">
            @if podcasts|length > 0
                @for podcast in podcasts
                        @include 'podcasts/_podcast.html'
                @endfor
            @else
                    No podcasts matching the search terms
```

```
            @endif
        </div>
@endblock
```

This is from `resources/templates/podcasts/search.html`.

Since we're making the list of podcasts dynamic, we've created a `PodcastController` method to return that list. It's returning an empty array, for now, but we'll expand it over time.

That array is passed to the `podcasts/search.html` template, by supplying a dictionary to `view.render`. Then, in the template, we replace the preview static content with a bit of dynamic code. We check to see if there are any podcasts, failing which we render some helpful text.

If there are podcasts, we loop over them. There are loads of things going on here, so we're going to spend some time looking at what this template is doing and what templates can do in general. Buckle up!

Template Conditionals

Masonite templates are a superset of Jinja2 templates. That means, anything you can do in an ordinary Jinja2 template you can do in Masonite. Masonite includes some extra goodies, like the alternate block syntax.

Here are some ways you can interact with data from the controller:

1. **If statements**

    These are the simplest checks we can do, inside a template. They take a variable or expression which doesn't need to be a Boolean. The value of the variable or expression is interpreted as either `True` or `False`. If `True`, the nested block will be displayed.

    When we say `@if podcasts|length > 0`, we're saying "if the number of podcasts is greater than zero, show the next nested level of content." We can also define an `@else` block and multiple `@elif` blocks.

I personally don't like the idea of using @elif blocks, as they tend to make templates messy very quickly. It's far clearer to define multiple templates and to do as much conditional logic as is practical inside the controller.

2. **Loop statements**

   These help us to render a block of content/markup for each item in a list. In our example application, we may use them to render a list of podcasts, as we're doing in the preceding example.

   Notice the difference between @endfor and @endif. These help the compiler to know which kind of conditional block is being closed, so it's important to use the appropriate closing block. It's something that takes getting used to, especially since Python doesn't have block terminators like this.

3. **Include statements**

   These are useful for including other templates into the current one. We could, for instance, put the block we render for each podcast into another template and include it inside the loop.

   The included template has access to all the variables defined in the template which includes it. We don't need to "pass them down" or anything. We can just start using them straight away.

4. **Extend/block statements**

   These are great for extending an existing layout, as we learned about in Chapter 3. We're going to learn more about blocks, as we add more JavaScript to our application.

You can see more details in the official documentation: Views - Masonite Documentation.

Template Filters

In addition to what you can do, using Masonite block syntax, there are a bunch of filters which Jinja2 ships with:

1. **value|'default'**

   When we get around to showing podcast details, we'll see this filter used more. It says, "if the `value` is not false, show it. Otherwise, show the value `'default'`." It's great for filling the gaps where there is no content to show.

2. **items|first**

   This filter shows the first item from a list of items. It's useful if you have a list of things, but you only want to show the first. Of course, you could always pull the first item out the list, in the controller, and only send that to the view.

3. **'hello %s'|format(name)**

   This filter works like the Python string interpolation method. It's useful if you want to use a template string inside the template, and you have access to variables you want to replace placeholders with.

4. **items|join(' , ')**

   This filter helps to combine a list of items into a single string, using another string to go between each item. If the list is only one item long, the "join" string won't be added at all.

5. **items|last**

   Similar to `first` but it returns the last item.

6. **items|length**

   This filter returns the length of a list of items. It's essential for pagination and summarizing list contents in search results.

7. **items|map(attribute='value') or items|map('lower')|join(',')**

    map is an extremely powerful filter. With it, we can pluck attributes out of each object in a list or provide another filter to be applied for each item in a list. Then it can even be combined, by extracting an attribute and then applying another filter to each extracted value.

8. **items|random**

    Returns a random item from a longer list of items.

9. **value|reverse**

    Reverses n object (like a string), or returns an iterator that traverses the items in a list in reverse.

10. **items|sort or items|sort(attribute='name',reverse=True)**

    This filter sorts a list of items. If the items are strings, just using |sort should be enough, though you might also want to change the reverse parameter to make it sort descending. If the items are dictionaries, you can select which attribute to sort by.

11. **value|trim**

    Trims the whitespace before and after a string.

There are quite a few filters not covered in this list. I think some of them are simple but not as useful, while others are a bit more in-depth that I'd like us to go at this point. If you're searching for a filter you don't see here, check out the Jinja2 filter documentation: `https://jinja.palletsprojects.com/en/2.10.x/templates/#list-of-builtin-filters`.

CSRF Protection

One thing I want to mention, before we look at how to use this form on the back end, is the `{{ csrf_field }}` field. CSRF (or **C**ross-**S**ite **R**equest **F**orgery) is a security concern that arises when you start to use forms on your site.

Web applications, which require users to log in to perform sensitive operations, might store some of those credentials in the browser. That way, when you navigate from page to page (or when you return to the site after a while), you are still logged in.

The problem with this is that malicious folks can forge a request from you to the web application that requires authentication. Imagine you are logged in to Facebook, in your browser. While you're browsing an unrelated site, that site uses an Ajax request to navigate your browser to the Facebook URL that causes your account to follow theirs.

That can't happen because Facebook is using a thing called CSRF protection. It adds a special token to the page from which your account could naturally follow another account. Then, when your browser initiates the request to follow another account, Facebook compares the token it has remembered for you with the token the HTTP request passed along.

If they match, your browser must have proceeded through a natural path to initiate the follow operation.

I don't want to dwell too much on the details of this, except to say that Masonite provides a simple mechanism to use the same security Facebook uses. `{{ csrf_field }}` creates a hidden field, which holds this CSRF token. If your forms don't use `{{ csrf_field }}`, you probably won't be able to submit their contents to another Masonite URL, by default.

To a lesser degree, CSRF protection also makes it harder for automation scripts (or bots) to use your web application. They have to do double the number of requests and adapt to changes in the markup of the page where they find the initial token.

CSRF can affect web applications that perform destructive or sensitive operations through HTTP GET requests. It's just that good applications seldom perform these kinds of operations through GET requests, because that goes against the original design of the HTTP specification. You should do the same.

In Chapter 2, we glimpsed CSRF, while we were adding exceptions to some middleware. It's important to remember that, while we shouldn't make a habit of it, we definitely can bypass this built-in CSRF protection. If there are HTTP endpoints we want to "open up" to other services, we can do so by adding them to the CSRF middleware exceptions list:

```
"""CSRF Middleware."""

from masonite.middleware import CsrfMiddleware as Middleware
```

```python
class CsrfMiddleware(Middleware):
    """Verify CSRF Token Middleware."""

    exempt = [
            '/home',
            '/home/@name',
            '/paypal/notify',
    ]

    very_request = False
    token_length = 30
```

This is from app/http/middleware/CsrfMiddleware.py.

A really good example of this is that services like PayPal and Stripe will, at our request, send us details about payments made by our customers. We're not going to be using them, for our home automation, but you're likely to encounter something similar the more you build.

Services like these need a way to send us HTTP POST requests, without jumping through the CSRF hoop. They're not first going to open a form in a browser and find the CSRF token.

The trick is being specific about which endpoints are allowed to bypass the built-in protection and making sure they are bulletproof.

What happens when people call these endpoints with a valid user session in the browser? What about when they call the endpoints with malicious data? What about when the endpoint is hammered by bots?

These are the questions you should ask, before allowing an endpoint to bypass the protection.

Validating Form Data

Once the form is submitted, we need to check that the data it provides is valid. You could do this in the same controller action you used to display the search page, but I suggest you split these actions up a bit.

It's much easier to figure out where a change needs to happen when you're not combining multiple HTTP request methods and paths into the same action.

```
from masonite.request import Request
from masonite.validation import Validator

# ...snip

def get_podcasts(self, query="):
    if query:
        dd(query)

    return []

def do_search(self, view: View, request: Request,
                    validate: Validator):
    errors = request.validate(
        validate.required('terms')
    )

    if errors:
        request.session.flash('errors', errors)
        return request.back()
        return view.render('podcast.search', {
            'podcasts': self.get_podcasts(request.input('terms'))
        })
```

This is from app/http/controllers/PodcastController.py.

Masonite ships with a powerful validation class, one that we'll undoubtedly reuse through this book. This is the simplest way to use it:

1. We type hint the Request and Validator parameters to our search action. Masonite's container, which we learned about in Chapter 3, reflects over the parameters to see which objects it should inject into the function call.

2.   We use the `validate` method, of the `Request` class, with a list of validations we want to perform. The `Validator` class provides different rule-generating methods we can use to define what valid data looks like.

3.   If there are errors, we find a reasonable way to notify the user of these errors. Flashing them to the session, which we learned about in Chapter 2, allows us to remember them temporarily. Then, after the redirect, we can display them for the user.

```
@if session().has('errors')
    <div class="bg-red-100 px-2 pt-2 pb-1 mb-2">
        @for field in session().get('errors')
            <div class="mb-1">
                {{ session().get('errors')[field]|join('. ') }}
            </div>
        @endfor
    </div>
@endif
```

This is from `resources/templates/podcasts/search.html`.

If there are validation errors, we want to be able to show them in the search template. Here, we have access to a `session()` function, which is a shortcut to the same `request.session` object we see in the controller.

If the session has an `errors` value, we show an enumeration of the fields it contains errors for. In a simple array, `@for item in items` will return values we can put directly into markup. For dictionaries, it becomes `@for key in items`. Each key is the name of a field with failed validation.

We then dereference those errors (where each field name, or key, has an array of error messages) and join them with the `join` filter we just learned about.

73

There are many built-in validation methods. So many, in fact, that I'd prefer we uncover them as we progress through the book instead of all at once. If you can't wait, head over to the official documentation to learn more: `https://docs.masoniteproject.com/advanced/validation`.

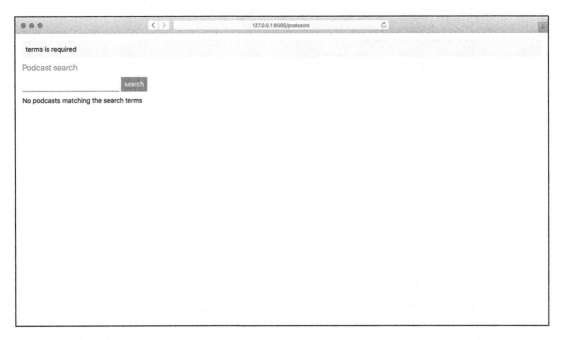

Figure 4-2. *Rendering error messages in a template*

Fetching Remote Data

Now that we're getting and validating search terms, it's time to fetch a list of matching podcasts. We'll tap into iTunes to find new podcasts and parse their data.

To begin with, we'll need a library to make remote requests:

```
pip install requests
```

In Chapter 3, we learned about creating service providers. Let's recap what we learned.

First, we created a new class, using a `craft` command:

```
craft provider RssParserProvider
```

We registered this, in config:

```
# ...snip

from app.providers.RssParserProvider import RssParserProvider

PROVIDERS = [
        # ...snip
        RssParserProvider,

]
```

This is from `config/providers.py`.

This new provider bound a parser class to the IoC container:

```
from masonite.provider import ServiceProvider
from app.helpers.RssParser import RssParser

class RssParserProvider(ServiceProvider):
    wsgi = False

    def register(self):
        self.app.bind('RssParser', RssParser())

    def boot(self):
        pass
```

This is from app/providers/RssParserProvider.py.

And, this RssParser class used a third-party library, called feedparser (https://pythonhosted.org/feedparser/index.html), to parse a feed URL:

```
import feedparser

class RssParser:
    def parse(url):
        return feedparser.parse(url)
```

This is from app/helpers/RssParser.py.

We're going to repeat the process when we bind an HTTP requests library to the IoC container. We'll use a library called Requests (https://2.python-requests.org/en/master), beginning with the new provider:

```
craft provider HttpClientProvider
```

Then, we need to bind an HttpClient inside that provider:

```
from masonite.provider import ServiceProvider
from app.helpers.HttpClient import HttpClient

class HttpClientProvider(ServiceProvider):
    wsgi = False

def register(self):
    self.app.bind('HttpClient', HttpClient())

    def boot(self):
        pass
```

This is from app/providers/HttpClientProvider.py.

We also need to add this provider to config:

```
# ...snip
from app.providers import (
    HttpClientProvider,
    RssParserProvider
)

PROVIDERS = [
        # ...snip
        HttpClientProvider,
        RssParserProvider,
]
```

This is from config/providers.py.

This kind of import shorthand is only possible if we also create an init__ file:

```
from .HttpClientProvider import HttpClientProvider
from .RssParserProvider import RssParserProvider
```

This is from app/providers/init.py.

The HttpClient class is just a proxy to the requests library:

```
import requests


class HttpClient:
    def get(*args):
            return requests.get(*args)
```

This is from app/helpers/HttpClient.py.

Resolving Dependencies from the Container

Now that we have these tools at our disposal, we need to get them out of the container, so we can use them to search for new podcasts:

```
from masonite.controllers import Controller
from masonite.request import Request
from masonite.validation import Validator
from masonite.view import View

class PodcastController(Controller):
    def __init__ (self, request: Request):
        self.client = request.app().make('HttpClient')
        self.parser = request.app().make('RssParser')

    def show_search(self, view: View):
        return view.render('podcasts.search', {
            'podcasts': self.get_podcasts()
        })

    def get_podcasts(self, query="):
        if query:
            dd([query, self.client, self.parser])

        return []
```

```
def do_search(self, view: View, request: Request,
                          validate: Validator):
    errors = request.validate(
        validate.required('terms')
    )

    if errors:
        request.session.flash('errors', errors)
        return request.back()

    return view.render('podcasts.search', {
        'podcasts': self.get_podcasts(
            request.input('terms')
        )
    })
```

This is from app/http/controllers/PodcastController.py.

We've added an init__ method, which resolves HttpClient and RssParser out of the container.

This isn't the only way to resolve these dependencies, and the alternatives definitely deserve some consideration. We'll circle back to them before too long.

Now, all that remains is to make the iTunes request and parse the results of a search:

```
def get_podcasts(self, query="):
    if query:
        response = self.client.get(
            'https://itunes.apple.com/search?media=podcast&term=' +
            query)
        return response.json()['results']

    return []
```

This is from app/http/controllers/PodcastController.py.

iTunes provides a neat, open HTTP endpoint, through which we can search for new podcasts. The only thing that remains is for us to format the data we get back from this endpoint:

```html
<div class="w-full md:w-2/5 mr-2 flex flex-row pb-2">
     <div class="min-h-full w-48"

style="background-image: url('{{podcast.artworkUrl600}}');
background-size: 100% auto; background-repeat: no-repeat;
background-position: center center; "></div>
        <div class="p-4 flex flex-col flex-grow">
             <div class="mb-8 flex flex-col flex-grow">
                  <div class="text-xl mb-2">
{{ podcast.collectionName }}</div>
                    <!-- <p class="text-base">description</p> -->
             </div>
             <div class="flex flex-grow items-center">
                  <!-- <div class="w-10 h-10 bg-red-300"></div> -->
                  <div class="text-sm">
                       <p class="leading-none">
{{ podcast.artistName }}</p>
                         <!-- <p class="">date</p> -->
                  </div>
           </div>
     </div>
</div>
```

This is from `resources/templates/podcasts/_podcast.html`.

I've commented out some of the fields, because we'd need to parse each podcast's RSS feed to find that information. That's definitely possible now that we can pull the RSS feed parser from the IoC container, but I feel like we've achieved enough for this chapter, already.

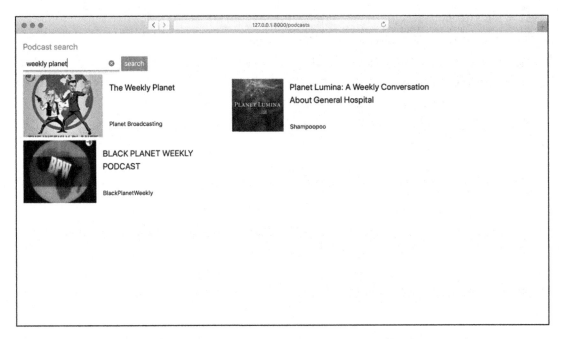

Figure 4-3. *Finding new podcasts, in an app we built!*

Summary

We covered a lot of things in this chapter. There's also a lot of things we could add. Consider it a challenge to find out more information, about each podcast, and fill out the _podcast.html template a bit more.

Aside from learning all about forms and templates, we also got a chance to further cement what we learned about the IoC container and how to add our own services to it.

In the next chapter, we're going to explore how to persist this kind of data to a database, and all that entails.

## CHAPTER 5

Using a Database

In the previous chapter, we learned all about forms. We created a few and even made them fetch data from remote sources. That's useful, but not as much unless we can also store and retrieve data from our own data sources. So, in this chapter, we're going to learn about how to set up a database, how to store data in it, and how to pull that same data back out of it.

How Do I Store Data?

I've already hinted at one way, but in truth there are many other ways to store and retrieve data. We could go "old school" and use flat files of XML or JSON data. It's certainly one of the simplest ways, but it suffers from problems like file locks and limited distribution.

We could use something like Firebase, which is still a database, but it's not one we have to manage and control. It also costs more than just using a database on the same server. It's a bit harder to administer, and it's not as fast as it *could* be.

Instead, we'll use a local MySQL database (and some SQL to boot) in order to store our data. Masonite has great support for MySQL databases and even some tools to help us structure our database. This is going to be fun!

Keeping the Database in Code

This code can be found at `https://github.com/assertchris/friday-server/tree/chapter-6`.

© Christopher Pitt and Joe Mancuso 2020
C. Pitt and J. Mancuso, *The Definitive Guide to Masonite*, https://doi.org/10.1007/978-1-4842-5602-2_5

Usually, at this point in a book, the author might ask you to step out to another application. They might ask you to start planning and building your database directly and completely disconnect from your code editor. I'm not going to ask you to do that for a couple reasons:

1. I believe database can and should be represented in the code of your application, because that's where they are tested, and that's the number one place you need to understand them.

2. Masonite provides tools to do it. All the frameworks I like to use provide these tools. It's a solved problem!

Let's say we wanted to start storing podcasts (as the result of "subscribing" to them, through our existing UI). We might decide to store those podcast URLs, together, in the users table. Perhaps in a text field, and delimited by commas.

Alternatively, we might want to create a new table and call it subscriptions. This second approach feels a lot cleaner, to me, as some users may not even want to subscribe to podcasts in the first place. They might want to listen to music, instead!

To get started, we need to create a thing called a migration, using craft:

```
craft migration create_subscriptions_table
```

This will create a new, and empty, migration:

```python
from orator.migrations import Migration

class CreateSubscriptionsTable(Migration):
    def up(self):
        """Run the migrations."""
        pass

    def down(self):
        """Revert the migrations."""
        pass
```

This is from database/migrations/x_create_subscriptions_table.py.

There are two parts to a migration:

1. up – Where new additions/changes are made to the existing database structure

2. down – Where these new additions/changes can be rolled back, in case there's a problem or the migration happened too soon

Let's define a new table:

```python
from orator.migrations import Migration

class CreateSubscriptionsTable(Migration):
    def up(self):
        with self.schema.create('subscriptions') as table:
            table.increments('id')
            table.string('url')
            table.string('title')
            table.timestamps()

    def down(self):
        self.schema.drop('subscriptions')
```

This is from database/migrations/x_create_subscriptions_table.py.

To begin with, our subscriptions table is kinda small and simple. We're going to store the title of a podcast and the URL where the podcast details may be found. We create a table by calling the schema.create method. This returns a new table object, which we can call various methods on, to create fields for in the table.

There are a few fields which are quite common and important:

1. increments – An auto-number integer field, which is the primary key for the table

2. timestamps – A couple timestamp fields, to remember when certain events took place (like when the record was created to last updated)

There are many other field types, too:

1. `string` – A length-limited string field

2. `text` – A variable-length string field

3. `integer` – An integer field

4. `float` – A decimal field

5. `timestamp` – A timestamp field

Fields may also have modifiers on them, which affect the metadata of the field. We could apply one of these, for instance:

1. `nullable` – When the field is allowed to contain NULL as a value

2. `default(value)` – For the default value a non-nullable field should have

3. `unsigned` – For any of the numeric fields, so they can store twice as many nonnegative numbers

---

There are quite a few field types I've not mentioned here. You can refer to the Orator documentation, if you're looking for something that's missing. Orator is the name of the underlying database library, which makes all of this possible.

Creating new tables is one reason to make a migration, but you might also want to change the structure of a table. In that case, you'd use the `schema.table` method:

```
from orator.migrations import Migration

class ChangeSubscriptionsTable(Migration):
    def up(self):
        with self.schema.table('subscriptions') as table:
            table.string('title', 200).change()

    def down(self):
        with self.schema.table('subscriptions') as table:
            table.string('title').change()
```

This is from database/migrations/x_change_subscriptions_table.py.

Aside from changing a field, this is also a good example of how to use the down method. The idea is that anything you add to or change in the database is "reverted" in the down method. We changed the title field to be length limited, so the rollback of this would be to remove that 200-character limit.

Similarly, we could also call a `table.dropColumn(name)` method to remove a field or a `schema.drop(name)` method to drop the table entirely.

It takes a bit of time to come around to this way of thinking about database tables. I encourage you to take a read through the Orator documentation, for managing migrations, so you can get familiar with all the different things you can do in a migration.

Before we can run these migrations, we probably need to make sure everything is set up. You should have a MySQL database installed. If you're on macOS (and have Homebrew installed), you can do this:

```
brew install mysql
```

For other systems and configurations, check out the Orator configuration documentation.

You'll also need to install one of the database dependencies:

```
pip install mysqlclient
```

Finally, you'll need to make sure your `.env` database credentials match up to a database you've already created:

```
DB_DATABASE=Friday
DB_USERNAME=<username>
DB_PASSWORD=<password>
```

Homebrew uses **username "root"** and **password ""** by default. These are not what I'd call secure credentials, but it's good to know about them if this is the first time you're using MySQL on your system. You can, of course, change them to suit your needs. Even with these credentials, you'll still need to make sure MySQL is running and that you've created a database to match the one you've configured.

Filling the Database with Dummy Data

Some folks test their applications with an empty database, or by manually inserting data by using the site. This can be a bit of a trap, because it means the data that they insert conforms to how they expect the site to be used, and seldom covers all the important states a particular part of the app can be in. Let's think about some of the different states our application could be in:

- The empty search screen, before we search for a podcast

- The empty search screen, when no results are found

- A "details" screen, showing the particulars of a podcast

- A "subscriptions" screen, showing all the podcasts someone is subscribed to

- An empty "subscriptions" screen, when the user hasn't subscribed to any podcasts

Not to mention all the confirmation screens, for subscribing and unsubscribing to podcasts.

And, this is just one data type in what might become a huge application! Imagine trying to test all these things manually. You'd probably forget about half the pages, and the manual testing would take ages (or just not happen).

Beyond these problems, imagine the kinds of data you'd have in the app:

- Would you cater for podcasts with huge titles?

- Would you cater for search results numbering in the hundreds?

- Could your application handle Unicode characters in podcast titles?

Filling the database with test data (or seeding, as it's commonly referred to) is an important **design** step, because it helps you remember all the edge cases and states you need to think about. When combined with testing (which we'll get to in Chapter 15), seed data forces a design to be robust.

The question becomes: How do we seed database data? There's a craft command for that:

```
craft seed subscriptions
```

This creates a new seed(er) file, which looks like this:

```
from orator.seeds import Seeder

class SubscriptionsTableSeeder(Seeder):
    def run(self):
        pass
```

This is from `database/seeds/subscriptions_table_seeder.py`.

We can change this, slightly, so that we're sure it's running:

```
from orator.seeds import Seeder
class SubscriptionsTableSeeder(Seeder):
    def run(self):
        print('in the seeder')
```

This is from `database/seeds/subscriptions_table_seeder.py`.

Before this will run, we need to add it to the "base" seeder:

```
from orator.seeds import Seeder
# from .user_table_seeder import UserTableSeeder
from .subscriptions_table_seeder import SubscriptionsTableSeeder

class DatabaseSeeder(Seeder):
    def run(self):
        # self.call(UserTableSeeder)
        self.call(SubscriptionsTableSeeder)
```

This is from `database/seeds/database_seeder.py`.

This seeder is the entry point through which craft will run all the other seeders. I have commented out the user stuff, because we don't need it until Chapter 8. I have also added the subscriptions seeder and called it using the `self.call` method.

Let's seed the database, to see if the subscriptions seeder is running:

```
craft seed:run
> in the seeder
> Seeded: SubscriptionsTableSeeder
> Database seeded!
```

If you also see the "in the seeder" text, then the subscriptions seeder is working. Let's learn a bit about how to read from and write to the database.

Writing to the Database

It would be helpful to have a database UI application running, so you can see the things we're about to do to the database. I highly recommend TablePlus or Navicat. If you're looking for something cheaper, check out HeidiSQL.

We're about to learn how to interact with a database, and Orator will generate and use SQL to do this. You don't need to know SQL, but it will undoubtedly help. Check out the books Apress has on the subject at www.apress.com/us/databases/mysql.

Let's begin writing to the database by faking a subscription. Our subscriptions table has a couple material fields we need to fill in:

```python
from config.database import DB
from orator.seeds import Seeder

class SubscriptionsTableSeeder(Seeder):
    def run(self):
        DB.table('subscriptions').insert({
            'url': 'http://thepodcast.com',
            'title': 'The podcast you need to listen to',
        })
```

This is from database/seeds/subscriptions_table_seeder.py.

The database connection is defined in the config section of our application, and we can pull the connection instance from there, to write to it. If you've got your database GUI open, you should now see a subscription in the subscriptions table. You should also see the corresponding SQL statement in the console.

It's useful that we don't need to write the full SQL statement out in order for it to be executed. This is a side effect of Orator trying to build SQL statements that work in any of the engines it supports. The idea is that we should be able to move to a different (supported) engine, and all our abstracted SQL statements should continue to work.

There are other kinds of operations we can do, but we'll get to examples of those in a bit.

This code is only the first step. If we want our seeders to be really helpful (and our designs to be robust), we need to use randomized data in the seeding phase. Orator installs a package, automatically, called Faker. It's a random fake data generator, which we can use in our seeder:

```python
from config.database import DB
from faker import Faker
from orator.seeds import Seeder

class SubscriptionsTableSeeder(Seeder):
    def run(self):
        fake = Faker()

        DB.table('subscriptions').insert({
            'url': fake.uri(),
            'title': fake.sentence(),
        })
```

This is from database/seeds/subscriptions_table_seeder.py.

Now, we can be prepared for different kinds and amounts of data in our designs, because we don't control exactly what data goes into them. We're not only populating them in ways that we expect the data to look. There are quite a few useful data types Faker provides, so I'm not going to go into them all. Sufficed to say, the Faker documentation is amazing, and you should definitely check it out: `https://faker.readthedocs.io/en/stable/providers.html`.

Reading from the Database

Inserting data is cool, but how do we get the data back out of the database, so that we can display it in the parts of the application that need it? Let's make a page to list the subscriptions we have.

```python
from config.database import DB
# ...snip

class PodcastController(Controller):
    # ...snip

    def show_subscriptions(self, view: View):
        subscriptions = DB.table('subscriptions').get()
        return view.render('podcasts.subscriptions', {
            'subscriptions': subscriptions,
        })
```

This is from app/http/controllers/PodcastController.py.

```
@extends 'layout.html'

@block content
    <h1 class="pb-2">Subscriptions</h1>
    <div class="flex flex-row flex-wrap">
        @if subscriptions|length > 0
            @for subscription in subscriptions
                @include 'podcasts/_subscription.html'
            @endfor
```

```
        @else
            No subscriptions
        @endif
    </div>
@endblock
```

This is from `resources/templates/podcasts/subscriptions.html`.

```
<div class="w-full flex flex-col pb-2">
    <div class="text-grey-darker">{{ subscription.title }}</div>
    <div class="text-sm text-grey">{{ subscription.url }}</div>
</div>
```

This is from `resources/templates/podcasts/_subscription.html`.

```
RouteGroup(
    [
        # ...snip
        Get('/subscriptions',
            'PodcastController@show_subscriptions').name('-show-
            subscriptions')
    ],
    prefix='/podcasts',
    name='podcasts',
),
```

This is from `routes/web.py`.

These four files should be more familiar to you now. The first is an additional controller action, which responds to the route we create in the fourth. The second and third files are the markup (views) to show the list of subscriptions. It should look something like Figure 5-1 in the browser.

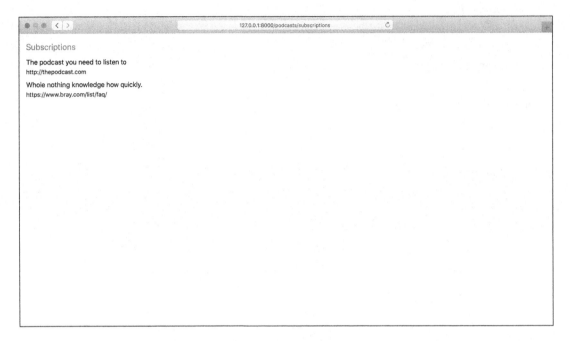

Figure 5-1. *Listing subscriptions stored in the database*

Hidden in that new controller action is the database code that pulls the subscriptions out of the database: `DB.table('subscriptions').get()`.

Filtering Database Data

What about if we want to filter that list? First we need to add fields to filter by. The most useful would be to add the ability to "favorite" a subscription, so that it appears at the top of the list. To this end, we need to create another migration:

```
from orator.migrations import Migration
class AddFavoriteToSubscriptionsTable(Migration):
    def up(self):
        with self.schema.table('subscriptions') as table:
            table.boolean('favorite').index()

    def down(self):
        with self.schema.table('subscriptions') as table:
            table.drop_column('favorite')
```

This is from database/migrations/x_add_favorite_to_subscriptions_
table.py.

In this new migration, we're adding a boolean field, called favorite, and making an index for it. The notes migration is reversed; we're also dropping this column, so that it's like it was never there. It may be useful to know that you can roll back all the migrations and run them all again, using craft:

```
craft migrate:refresh --seed
```

We may also need to update the seeder to account for this new field – since we aren't allowing the field to be nullable and we're also not specifying a default value:

```
from config.database import DB
from faker import Faker
from orator.seeds import Seeder

class SubscriptionsTableSeeder(Seeder):
    def run(self):
        fake = Faker()

        DB.table('subscriptions').insert({
            'url': fake.uri(),
            'title': fake.sentence(),
            'favorite': fake.boolean(),
        })
```

This is from database/seeds/subscriptions_table_seeder.py.

Now that we have a new filterable field, we can split the subscriptions into a list of "ordinary subscriptions" and "favorite subscriptions":

```
@extends 'layout.html'

@block content
    <h1 class="pb-2">Favorites</h1>
    <div class="flex flex-row flex-wrap">
```

```
        @if favorites|length > 0
            @for subscription in favorites
                @include 'podcasts/_subscription.html'
            @endfor
        @else
            No subscriptions
        @endif
    </div>
    <h1 class="pb-2">Subscriptions</h1>
    <div class="flex flex-row flex-wrap">
        @if subscriptions|length > 0
            @for subscription in subscriptions
                @include 'podcasts/_subscription.html'
            @endfor
        @else
            No subscriptions
        @endif
    </div>
@endblock
```

This is from `resources/templates/podcasts/subscriptions.html`.

We can duplicate the block of subscription-based code (and, maybe later, we can include the other one) so that we can use a different source of subscription items. We can call it favorites, but that also means we need to provide that from the controller:

```
def show_subscriptions(self, view: View):
    favorites = DB.table('subscriptions').where('favorite', True).get()
    subscriptions = DB.table('subscriptions').where(
        'favorite', '!=', True).get()

return view.render('podcasts.subscriptions', {
    'favorites': favorites,
    'subscriptions': subscriptions,
})
```

This is from `app/http/controllers/PodcastController.py`.

Here, we're using the `where` method to filter subscriptions by whether or not their favorite field has a truth value. It's one of the many useful query methods, including

- `where` with two arguments, where the first is the field and the second is the value

- `where` with three arguments, where the middle argument is the comparison operator (like how we're using `!=` to say "not equal to")

- `where_exists` with a single query object, so that the outer query only returns results when the inner query does (similar to a left join)

- `where_raw` with a raw where clause string (like `subscriptions.favorite = 1`)

There are some subtitles to these, which you can find by reading the documentation at `https://orator-orm.com/docs/0.9/query_builder.html#advanced-where`. It's not really important to remember exact syntax, but rather to be aware that these methods exist so that you know where in the documentation to go to learn more about them.

If we were to make the favorite field nullable, then the second query would catch all records where favorite wasn't set to `True`, including records where favorite was `False` and `Null`. We could be a bit more explicit, by saying `where('favorite', False)`, but we'd have to remember to change that if we ever made the favorite field nullable.

Updating Database Data

Let's add the ability to favorite (and unfavorite) a database record. We'll need a couple new controller actions and routes:

```python
def do_favorite(self, request: Request):
    DB.table('subscriptions').where('id', request.param('id')).update({
        'favorite': True,
    })

    return request.redirect_to('podcasts-show-subscriptions')
```

```
def do_unfavorite(self, request: Request):
    DB.table('subscriptions').where('id', request.param('id')).update({
        'favorite': False,
    })

    return request.redirect_to('podcasts-show-subscriptions')
```

This is from app/http/controllers/PodcastController.py.

In addition to an insert method, we can also use an update method to affect database records. These two actions are quite similar, but I think it best not to abstract them into a single method, because this is undeniably clear as to which action does what.

After updating the subscription, we're also redirecting back to the subscriptions page. We need to set up routes and change the subscription include:

```
from masonite.routes import Get, Patch, Post, Match, RouteGroup

ROUTES = [
    # ...snip

    RouteGroup(
        [
            # ...snip

            Patch('/subscriptions/@id/favorite', 'PodcastController@do_
            favorite').name('-favorite- subscription'),
            Patch('/subscriptions/@id/unfavorite', 'PodcastController@do_
            unfavorite').name('-unfavorite- subscription'),
        ],
        prefix='/podcasts',
        name='podcasts',
    ),
]
```

This is from routes/web.py.

```
<div class="w-full flex flex-col pb-2">
    <div class="text-grey-darker">{{ subscription.title }}</div>
    <div class="text-sm text-grey">{{ subscription.url }}</div>
    <div class="text-sm text-grey">
        <form class="inline-flex" action="{{ route('podcasts-favorite-
          subscription', {'id': subscription.id}) }}" method="POST">
            {{ csrf_field }}
            {{ request_method('PATCH') }}
            <button onclick="event.preventDefault(); this.form.
              submit()">favorite</button>
        </form>
        <form class="inline-flex" action="{{ route('podcasts-unfavorite-
          subscription', {'id': subscription.id}) }}" method="POST">
            {{ csrf_field }}
            {{ request_method('PATCH') }}
            <button onclick="event.preventDefault(); this.form.
              submit()">unfavorite</button>
        </form>
    </div>
</div>
```

This is from `resources/templates/podcasts/_subscription.html`.

Since we're using non-GET and non-POST request methods (for the routes), we need to use forms to initiate the favorite/unfavorite actions. We tell Masonite that these are PATCH requests using the `request_method` view helper. We *should* be able to use the buttons to toggle a subscription between the lists we've created.

Deleting Database Data

The last bit of functionality I want us to add is the ability to unsubscribe from a podcast.

This requires little more code than we've already made and learned about:

```
<form class="inline-flex" action="{{ route('podcasts-unsubscribe', {'id':
subscription.id}) }}" method="POST">
    {{ csrf_field }}
    {{ request_method('DELETE') }}
    <button onclick="event.preventDefault(); this.form.
     submit()">unsubscribe</button>
</form>
```

This is from `resources/templates/podcasts/_subscription.html`.

This resembles our PATCH routes, but the appropriate method we need (for an "unsubscribe") is DELETE. Similarly, we need to use the `Delete` route method, when defining the route:

```
from masonite.routes import Delete, Get, Patch, Post, Match, RouteGroup

ROUTES = [
    # ...snip

    RouteGroup(
        [
            # ...snip

            Delete('/subscriptions/@id/unsubscribe', 'PodcastController
            @do_unsubscribe').name('-unsubscribe'),
        ],
        prefix='/podcasts',
        name='podcasts',
    ),
]
```

This is from `routes/web.py`.

And, we can use the `delete` method to remove the record from the subscriptions table:

```
def do_unsubscribe(self, request: Request):
    DB.table('subscriptions').where('id', request.param('id')).delete()

    return request.redirect_to('podcasts-show-subscriptions')
```

This is from `app/http/controllers/PodcastController.py`.

There is so much depth to this part of Masonite that no single chapter can ever do it justice. This has been a taste, but the only way you're going to get to grips with all that Orator has to offer, here, is to dig deep into the document and to actually use Orator to do different and complex things.

You can find detailed documentation, for these DB statements, at `https://orator-orm.com/docs/0.9/query_builder.html#introduction`.

Simplifying Code Through Models

Now that we have a handle on writing abstracted database queries, I want us to look at how these can be simplified by the judicious use of models. Models are what we call objects that follow the Active Record database pattern. It's a bit of a tricky concept, at first. The basic idea is that we define database tables as classes, using static methods to refer to table-level actions and instance methods to refer to row-level actions.

We can define a new model, using craft:

```
craft model Subscription
```

This produces a new class, which looks like this:

```
from config.database import Model

class Subscription(Model):
    """Subscription Model."""
    pass
```

This is from app/Subscription.py.

This Subscription class extends the Orator Model class, which means it already has a lot of magic available to reduce the code we've already written. We can simplify our initial set of retrieval queries, by referring directly to the model:

```python
from app.Subscription import Subscription

# ...later

def show_subscriptions(self, view: View):
    # favorites = DB.table('subscriptions').where('favorite', True).get()

    favorites = Subscription.where('favorite', True).get()

    # subscriptions = DB.table('subscriptions').where(
    #     'favorite', '!=', True).get()

    subscriptions = Subscription.where(
        'favorite', '!=', True).get()

    return view.render('podcasts.subscriptions', {
        'favorites': favorites,
        'subscriptions': subscriptions,
    })
```

This is from app/http/controllers/PodcastController.py.

Similarly, we can simplify the seeding and updating and deleting by also referring directly to the model:

```python
from app.Subscription import Subscription
# from config.database import DB
from faker import Faker
from orator.seeds import Seeder
```

```
class SubscriptionsTableSeeder(Seeder):
    def run(self):
        fake = Faker()

        # DB.table('subscriptions').insert({
        #     'url': fake.uri(),
        #     'title': fake.sentence(),
        #     'favorite': fake.boolean(),
        # })

        Subscription.create(
            url=fake.uri(),
            title=fake.sentence(),
            favorite=fake.boolean(),
        )

        # ...or

        Subscription.create({
            'url': fake.uri(),
            'title': fake.sentence(),
            'favorite': fake.boolean(),
        })
```

This is from database/seeds/subscriptions_table_seeder.py.

The first time you run this, you're likely to encounter a MassAssignmentError. That's because Masonite protects against unintended bulk updates to records. We can bypass this by adding a special property to the model:

```
class Subscription(Model):
    __fillable__ = ['title', 'url', 'favorite']
```

This is from app/Subscription.py.

```
def do_favorite(self, request: Request):
    # DB.table('subscriptions').where('id', request.param('id')).update({
    #     'favorite': True,
    # })

    subscription = Subscription.find(request.param('id'))
    subscription.favorite = True
    subscription.save()

    return request.redirect_to('podcasts-show-subscriptions')

def do_unfavorite(self, request: Request):
    # DB.table('subscriptions').where('id', request.param('id')).update({
    #     'favorite': False,
    # })

    subscription = Subscription.find(request.param('id'))
    subscription.favorite = False
    subscription.save()

    return request.redirect_to('podcasts-show-subscriptions')

def do_unsubscribe(self, request: Request):
    # DB.table('subscriptions').where('id', request.param('id')).delete()

    subscription = Subscription.find(request.param('id'))
    subscription.delete()

    return request.redirect_to('podcasts-show-subscriptions')
```

This is from app/http/controllers/PodcastController.py.

I've left the previous DB calls here, but commented out, so we can compare them to the model-based code. In some cases, it's slightly more code to use the model, but the results are much clearer. As we progress through the rest of the book, you're going to see much more model code and much less low-level query code.

Summary

In this chapter, we had our first look into how to use the database. We went all the way from defining database structure through to representing tables and rows in the form of models. It's been a bit of a whirlwind tour, but it's also foundational for the rest of the book.

Take some time to experiment with different database queries and actions, and see how they can be used in model form. Try creating a "subscribe" action, so that podcasts returned in search results are persisted to the database. If you can achieve that, given what you've learned in this chapter, then you're on a rocket ship to mastery of Masonite!

CHAPTER 6

Security

Masonite is developed with application security in mind. When a release is getting ready, it will be reviewed for any possible security vulnerabilities by a maintainer. Masonite also makes use of services such as DeepSource which will scan each pull request for possible security vulnerabilities, code smells, possible bugs, and other code issues.

It would be foolish to think all security vulnerabilities will never make it into the codebase, though, especially because of the fact that new ways to attack an application can be discovered or invented. There are other ways to handle situations like that, which we will talk about later in this chapter.

Another important reminder is that when we talk about Masonite and security, what we are really talking about is application security. Masonite is the application and we can only protect the application from vulnerabilities. There are many other types of vulnerabilities that Masonite cannot control. For example, there could be a vulnerability on your specific version of operating system that is hosting Masonite which can lead to an exploitation.

So it's important to note that just because your application is secure, it does not mean you are not vulnerable. You will need to learn many of the different avenues of attack and ensure you are protected.

CSRF Protection

CSRF stands for Cross-Site Request Forgery. In the simplest terms, it helps on two fronts:

- Protect against bad actors making requests on behalf of a user.

- Prevention against people sneaking in malicious code to your site to look like a button or an alert is coming from your site but it's really going to another site.

© Christopher Pitt and Joe Mancuso 2020
C. Pitt and J. Mancuso, *The Definitive Guide to Masonite*, https://doi.org/10.1007/978-1-4842-5602-2_6

Let's take the example of a login form. A user enters an email and a password and hits submit. The submission goes to an endpoint where we check if the username and password are correct and we login the user. But what prevents someone from simply sending a POST request to that page? Anybody can now just brute force their way by hitting the endpoint over and over via Postman or cURL.

The other protection is by preventing malicious code from being saved into a database and later displayed on your site. If someone can save a JavaScript `<script>` tag that simply hides your login button and displays their own login button except your input gets sent to their servers, then that would be devastating for security. Masonite, and, by extension, Orator and Jinja, protects against this attack by cleaning input every step of the way.

Let's talk more about how Masonite protects against these attacks.

Cleaning Request Input

By default, Masonite cleans request input for you so you do not have to worry about users submitting malicious JavaScript code. Masonite will clean out <,> and & characters. This is done all behind the scenes. So, for example, if we had this code snippet

```
"""
POST {
  'bad': '<script>alert('Give  me  your  bank  information')</script>'
}
"""
def show(self, request: Request):
  request.input('bad')
```

then we would actually get a value like

```
<script>alert(&#x27;Give me your bank information&#x27;)</script>
```

The HTML entities are now escaped and your browser will simply display this as text if it made it on to your web pages somewhere rather than execute the script.

You can choose not to clean something by passing in `clean=False`, but you are at your own risk if you choose to do this. By reading the rest of this chapter, you should be an expert on application security with Masonite.

The CSRF Token

We will be talking about a CSRF token a lot in this section, so let's dedicate a few paragraphs on talking about what it actually is and where it comes from.

The trick behind what the CSRF token is pretty simple: we give a token to the user and the user sends the token back. The token is just an unpredictable secret string given to the client and also known by the server. This allows the client to receive the token and send the token back. If the token we gave the client is not the same as the token we get back, then we will reject the request.

How do we know it came from our web site? Because the CSRF token is just a cookie registered to the user that came from our web site. In the beginning of the user's session (like when the user hit our site for the first time), a cookie was created called `csrf_token` which simply generated a completely random string which is our constant that we can check later.

When the user submits a form, they will also submit this CSRF token. We will take that token and check it against the one we saved in the cookie. If the cookie value and the value of the token they submitted both match, then we can make a very safe assumption that the user who had the cookie registered to them and the user who submitted the form are the same people.

Form Submissions

Masonite protects against CSRF attacks for form submissions. The CSRF flow described previously is exactly how CSRF protection on form submissions works.

```
<form action=".."  method="..">
  {{ csrf_field }}
  <input ..>
</form>
```

That {{ csrf_field }} you see in the form actually translates to

```
<input type="hidden" name=" token" value="906b697ba9dbc5675739b6fced6394">
```

when the page is fully rendered. Let's explain what this is doing because it's important.

First, it is creates a hidden input; this means it won't actually display on the form, but it will be there and it will submit this input in addition to the input that gets submitted from the user.

The second thing it's doing is actually submitting the CSRF token with the name of _token so we can fetch it from the back end to do our verification.

Lastly, it sets the value equal to the CSRF token. The CSRF token is generated once per user session by default (you can bump this up to every request later in the chapter).

When the user submits the form, it will check against the cookie and the user-submitted token and verify that they match. If it matches, it will let the request go through; if it does not, then it will block the request because if the values do not match, then the user either submitted the form maliciously or they manipulated the token values maliciously. Either way we block the request.

AJAX Calls

AJAX calls are a little different than form submissions. AJAX calls don't utilize the same type of request that forms submit. AJAX calls are typically done via JavaScript, do what's called an "asynchronous request," and expect a response back before redirecting or doing some other logic within JavaScript.

Because of this, the preceding approach with sending a hidden input no longer works. But don't worry because you can still send the token along with your request, but you would just send it within your Ajax call.

Similar to how you can use the {{ csrf_field }} built-in variable, you can use the {{ csrf_token }} variable to just get the token. We can then put that token inside a meta tag and put it into our head section of our HTML:

```
<head>
  <title>Page Title</title>
  <meta name="csrf-token" content="{{ csrf_token }}">
</head>
```

Now in order to get the token to pass along with our call, we can simply get the token from this meta field:

```
let token = document.head.querySelector('meta[name="csrf-token"]').content;
```

The rest is up to what JavaScript framework you are using. If you are using jQuery, it might look something like this:

```
let token = document.head.querySelector('meta[name="csrf-token"]').content;

$.ajax({
  type: "POST",
  data: {
    'email': 'user@example.com',
    'password': 'secret',
    '_token': token
  },
  success: success,
  dataType: dataType
});
```

Notice we are passing the _token along very similarly to how we were doing it with a form request, but now we need to pass it more manually.

Some people make the mistake of trying to use CSRF token between servers or between applications. Remember, CSRF tokens are only for use within the same application. If you need to make requests between applications or between servers, you should look into using JWT tokens and API authentication methods or something similar and not CSRF tokens.

Password Reset

If you are first starting a project, it is advised to run the craft auth command which will scaffold out several views, routes, and controllers for you which handles logging in, registering, authentication, and password resets. You don't need to do this, but it will prevent you from needing to build all of it out yourself and it's 100% customizable.

One of the most vulnerable parts of an application is the password reset functionality. Since this part of your application is handling sensitive data like a password, it is a ripe target for your malicious actors. Protecting your password resets is vital.

There are several different best approaches for resetting your password, but let's explain exactly how Masonite does it and we'll explain some key points along the way.

The Form

The first part of a password reset process is going to the password reset form. By default this is under the /password route if you are using the default scaffolding. The form is a submit input to enter the email and a simple submit button.

When the user enters their email and hits submit, we do a lookup of the email in our database, and if it exists, we send them an email using the email address we have in our database with a URL appended with a token. They will get a success notification back that an email has been sent to them and to follow the instructions there.

The second important piece you might have missed is that we send an email to the user's email we get from our database and we **do not send an email to the user's email they submitted**. In other words, we do a lookup of the user in our database with the email address that the user submitted, **but we send an email to the one in our database**. At first glance, this might seem strange; I mean, they are the same email address, right? Well not exactly. There are differences between Unicode characters and non-Unicode characters. To the blind eye, they might seem the same.

Unicode Attack

Let's talk about the Unicode attack which is one of the most dangerous attacks when it comes to password resets.

First, let's explain what a Unicode is. Each character in Unicode receives a number under the hood. The numbers get stored in the format of something like U+0348 and then can be decoded on all systems that support Unicode (which is nearly all systems). It's basically a character encoding standard. The issue is that some Unicode characters are remarkably similar to other Unicode characters.

Let's take these two email addresses:

```
John@Gɪthub.com
John@Github.com
```

Looks kind of similar, right? If you do a double take, you might realize something strange with the i in GitHub; there is no dot above it.

Let's try to do a comparison now:

```
>>> 'ı' == 'i'
False
```

Doing a comparison returns False, but now let's convert them both to upper:

```
>>> 'ı'.upper() == 'i'.upper()
True
```

This is because some Unicode characters have "Case Collisions," meaning when i is converted to uppercase and ı is converted to uppercase, they are both I. Now they match. What's even scarier is we can take the original email addresses we started with before and we can do the same comparison:

```
>>> 'John@Gıthub.com'.upper() == 'John@Github.com'.upper()
True
```

The email addresses are visually different but actually evaluate True. This is where the attack comes in.

A user can submit the email address John@Gıthub.com for a password reset; we could possibly find a match for John@Github.com in the database and then send an email address to the incorrect John@Gıthub.com address, thereby having an exploit in our password reset form.

This is why we make sure to send an email to the address we have in our database because it makes sure we are sending the reset instructions to the correct email address.

SQL Injection

Since we're already on the topic of attacks, we should also talk about another very common attack called SQL injection. This is probably the most common attack, and if you have been in software development for more than 5 minutes, you have heard of this.

SQL injection is actually really simple. SQL injection happens when you don't properly sanitize incoming user data and you then use that data to make queries. Let's take a simple code snippet of what might look like with Masonite and Orator:

```
def show(self, request: Request):
  User.where_raw(f"email = {request.input('email')}").first()
```

On a normal attempt, this could generate a query like this:

```
SELECT * FROM `users` WHERE `email` = 'user@example.com'
```

Seems pretty innocent, but that is assuming the request input is equal to user @example.com. What if it was equal to something more malicious, say, user@example.com; drop table users;?

Now that query looks something like

```
SELECT * FROM `users` WHERE `email` = user@example.com; drop table users;
```

This is actually now two queries. SQL will try to run the first query (and probably throw a syntax error) and then will try to run the second query, which is valid, and actually drop the users table.

The user now "injected" query into our database because we had a code vulnerability.

Query Binding

Notice in the preceding code example we used a raw query. I demonstrated this example because a code example might look like this:

```
def show(self, request: Request):
  User.where('email', request.input('email')).first()
```

In this example, the query is actually a bit different. Orator will now generate a query like this:

```
SELECT * FROM `users` WHERE `email` = ?
```

It will then send as part of a second step what the input is to the database. Underlying database packages will then be responsible for sanitizing the input to ensure nothing malicious is going on before sending to the database.

Mass Assignment

Orator has a very special kind of way of interacting with classes and databases. You'll notice that Orator models are extremely bare bones because Orator handles all the heavy lifting for you.

First, let's talk about the two methods that are actually mass assignment for Orator. Mass assignment is anything that updates a table from a bulk of inputs.

For example, these two lines of code are mass assignment:

```
def show(self, request: Request):
  User.create(request.all())
  User.find(1).update(request.all())
```

This code snippet is **not** mass assignment:

```
def show(self, request: Request):
  user = User.find(1)
  user.admin = request.input('is_admin')
  user.save()
```

The design pattern of Orator opens up the door to an attack called a mass assignment attack.

Let's take a look at this code snippet and then we'll walk through it:

```
"""
POST {
  'email': 'joe@masoniteproject.com',
  'name': 'Joe Mancuso',
  'password': 'secret'
}
"""
def show(self, request: Request):
  User.create(request.all())
```

If we have a simple request input, this query might look something like this:

```
INSERT INTO `users` (`email`, `name`, `password`)
  VALUES ('joe@masoniteproject.com', 'Joe Mancuso', 'secret')
```

This seems pretty innocent, but it leaves the door open for a user passing any information in. For example, they might pass in if they are an admin and all that they would have to do would be to pass those values in:

```
"""
POST {
  'email': 'joe@masoniteproject.com',
```

```
    'name': 'Joe Mancuso',
    'password': 'secret',
    'admin': 1
}
"""
def show(self, request: Request):
  User.create(request.all())
```

This would generate a query like this:

```
INSERT INTO `users` (`email`, `name`, `password`, `admin`)
  VALUES ('joe@masoniteproject.com', 'Joe Mancuso', 'secret', '1')
```

Now the user just made themselves an admin pretty simply.

Fillable

In order to protect against this attack, Orator made a __fillable__ property you can put on your model. Now we can do something like this:

```
class User:
    __fillable__ = ['email', 'name',  'password']
```

Now it will ignore any fields that try to get mass assigned. Going back to the vulnerable code snippet:

```
"""
POST {
  'email': 'joe@masoniteproject.com',
  'name': 'Joe Mancuso',
  'password': 'secret',
  'admin': 1
}
"""
def show(self, request: Request):
  User.create(request.all())
```

It will now correctly generate a query like this:

```
INSERT INTO `users` (`email`, `name`, `password`)
  VALUES ('joe@masoniteproject.com', 'Joe Mancuso', 'secret')
```

It will ignore everything that is not inside the __fillable__ property.

CORS

Most people interactions with CORS are from trying to access a server that implements CORS and then trying to get around CORS because people don't quite understand it.

CORS stands for Cross-Origin Resource Sharing and what it does is it allows servers to tell browsers through HTTP headers which specific resources are allowed to be accessed and how those resources should be accessed. For example, a server might tell a browser to only send requests to example.com if the request is coming from site.com. Maybe we have some kind of microservice and we want to make sure only applications from our application at site.com.

The way browsers handle this is they do something called a preflight request which is a simple HTTP request they send right before they send the payload. That preflight request is used to essentially "scout" the server and check if the CORS instructions match what they are about to send. If they do not match, then the browser will throw an error related to the CORS instructions not being valid.

This is not a surefire way to protect your application, but it does add a layer of security and request validation.

CORS Provider

Masonite allows your application to return CORS headers so we can help protect our application. To do so is pretty simple. We can simply add that provider to the provider configuration list right below your AppProvider:

```
# config/providers.py
# ...
from masonite.providers import CorsProvider
```

```
PROVIDERS = [
  AppProvider
  CorsProvider,
  # ...

]
```

Now your server will start returning the following CORS headers and browsers will start enforcing your rules.

Lastly you can add some sensible defaults to the bottom of your config/middleware.py file:

```
# config/middleware.py
# ...

CORS = {
    'Access-Control-Allow-Origin': "*",
    "Access-Control-Allow-Methods": "DELETE, GET, HEAD, OPTIONS, PATCH,
     POST, PUT",
    "Access-Control-Allow-Headers": "Content-Type, Accept, X-Requested-With",
    "Access-Control-Max-Age": "3600",
    "Access-Control-Allow-Credentials":  "true"
}
```

This will now set these headers when people visit your application:

```
Access-Control-Allow-Origin: *,
Access-Control-Allow-Methods: DELETE, GET, HEAD, OPTIONS, PATCH, POST, PUT,
Access-Control-Allow-Headers: Content-Type, Accept, X-Requested-With,
Access-Control-Max-Age: 3600,
Access-Control-Allow-Credentials: true
```

You can modify the headers by modifying the key and values of the CORS variable in your middleware file. You'll need to create this if you don't see it there:

```
# config/middleware.py
# ...
CORS = {
    "Access-Control-Allow-Origin": "*",
```

```
  "Access-Control-Allow-Methods": "DELETE, GET, HEAD, OPTIONS, PATCH,
    POST, PUT",
  "Access-Control-Allow-Headers": "Content-Type, Accept, X- Requested-With",
  "Access-Control-Max-Age": "3600",
  "Access-Control-Allow-Credentials": "true"
}
```

Feel free to modify these headers or even look up additional headers you can add.

Secure Headers

Similar to how CORS headers were for settings rules for HTTP requests made between origins, security headers set rules for all HTTP requests.

Some of the headers that Masonite has built in when using the SecureHeadersMiddleware middleware include

- Strict-Transport-Security

- X-Frame-Options

- X-XSS-Protection

- X-Content-Type-Options

- Referrer-Policy

- Cache-Control

- Pragma

These are pretty cryptic, so let's try to go over each one and explain what they are for. I won't go over what each value means since there are many of them. I'll just explain what each option is there for, and you can do the research on what values you need to set for your situation.

Meaning of the Headers

The Strict-Transport-Security header tells browser that it should make requests over HTTPS and not HTTP. This is also known as an HSTS header (**H**TTP **S**trict **T**ransport **S**ecurity).

The X-Frame-Options header tells a browser whether it should render pages inside <iframe>, <frame>, <embded>, or <object>. There have been known vulnerabilities with these options because a user can inject their own web sites into these iFrames. This could lead to users' credentials being stolen if they enter information into one of these hijacked frames. As long as your site is not vulnerable to CSRF, then you should be fine.

The X-XSS-Protection header tells the browser to block any requests if the browser itself detects any sign of cross-site scripting attacks.

The X-Content-Type-Options header prevents sniffing of MIME types (like images). Some MIME types contain executable code and then help prevent that.

The Referrer-Policy header details how much information should be available in the Referrer header when a request goes from your web page to another web page. Typically web sites can tell where a user just came from by reading this header.

The Cache-Control provides instructions to browsers on how much information and what type of information should be cached for both requests and responses.

Finally the Pragma Header is essentially the same thing as a Cache-Control header but used for backward compatibility.

Using the Secure Middleware

You can easily use this middleware by importing it into your config/middleware.py file:

```
from masonite.middleware import SecureHeadersMiddleware

HTTP_MIDDLEWARE = [
    # ...
    SecureHeadersMiddleware,
]
```

Also feel free to override any defaults by adding a SECURE_HEADERS variable at the bottom of the middleware configuration file:

```
from masonite.middleware import SecureHeadersMiddleware

HTTP_MIDDLEWARE = [
    # ...
    SecureHeadersMiddleware,
]
```

```
SECURE_HEADERS = {
    'X-Frame-Options' : 'deny'
}
```

Releases

When security vulnerabilities are found within the community, maintainers are made aware of it and a security release is created. These could be breaking changes inside minor releases which typically goes against release policy for Masonite, but an application breaking is better than user data being stolen or servers, applications, or databases being breached.

That is why it is important to be inside the community so everyone can know what is going on, and we can all try to be as transparent as possible when it is necessary to do so.

There will also be documentation on what the security release was, how we got here, and how to move forward. Some security releases can be done on Masonite's side by simply creating a new release, and some may need to be patched in the application itself.

When you are developing with Masonite, just be sure you are on the latest minor release. For example, if you are developing with Masonite 2.2, then be sure the third number is always up to date, like upgrading from 2.2.10 to 2.2.11. These are important to stay up to date. Minor releases are done sometimes every few days or every few weeks with no set schedule. Every so often you should check if Masonite created a release and what that release is, and you should upgrade and test before moving the changes out to a production server.

CVE Alerts

Since we are talking about releases and alerts, it's worth mentioning about CVE alerts. CVE stands for Common Vulnerabilities and Exposures. It is basically a giant archive of many exposures found within software. If a high-profile Python package has a discovered vulnerability, they will create a CVE which gets assigned an identification number everyone is able to reference.

If you are hosting your code on GitHub, then they will send you notifications when any of your packages correspond to a recently released CVE and will recommend solutions to fix. These should not be ignored, and if you are using the package with the vulnerability, you should upgrade or fix the issue as soon as possible.

Most solutions are a simple upgrade, but you should read the link to the document that is attached to it to see if your application was at risk and if any data could have potentially been exposed.

They even have a Twitter page @CVEnew if you want to follow them there.

Encryption

Encryption is a fun topic to talk about because it is the art of masking values and only allowing certain application, or users or servers, to see that value.

Masonite uses the famous cryptography package to do encryption. This package is pretty renowned in the Python community and there are an incredible amount of packages that require it.

Masonite uses the Fernet encryption algorithm from this package to do most encryption. Here is a section from their documentation on what Fernet is:

> *Fernet guarantees that a message encrypted using it cannot be manipulated or read without the key. Fernet is an implementation of symmetric (also known as "secret key") authenticated cryptography.*

You might have realized Masonite has a secret key. You could have seen it when Masonite was first installed, or you may have needed to generate one using the craft key command.

This secret key should **NEVER** be made public. If this key is made public, you should immediately generate a new secret key. There are many things in Masonite that are public facing and encrypted using this key, and if a malicious user got a hold of the key, then they would be able to decrypt some sensitive information.

Nothing in Masonite itself that is publically exposed like cookies has any sensitive information in it, but if you as a developer create a cookie with sensitive information in it (which you probably should not), then that information could be at risk.

You can find your key in your .env file, and it looks something like this:

```
-4gZFiEz_RQClTjr9CQMvgZfvO-YnTuO485GG_BMecs=
```

In fact, you should rotate out your key on a recurring basis if it will not do too much harm to your users. By default, the worst case scenario is that your users will be logged out because Masonite will delete any cookies it encrypted but cannot decrypt. With a new secret key, it will not be able to decrypt values it encrypted with a different key.

If this is ok for you, then you should rotate your key out possibly every week.

Encoding vs. Encryption

This is a VERY important topic to discuss here because many people don't know the difference. Something that is encoded typically uses some kind of standard encoding algorithm like Base64.

Encoded values are able to be decoded by anyone using virtually any program. Sensitive information should be not encoded; it should be encrypted.

Encryption typically uses an encryption via a secret key. This means that a value is converted (encrypted) into a hash and is not able to be decrypted back unless the same secret key to encrypt is used to decrypt it back.

Some encryption is called one-way encryption and can only be converted into a hash and **never** converted back. All lookups need to do the same one-way conversion into that same hash and check for similarities. Some one-way hashes are algorithms like MD5 and SHA1 which have since fallen out of favor for better available encryption algorithms.

So if I say either encryption or encoding, then be sure to refer to this section here if you don't know what I mean.

Password Encryption

Masonite uses Bcrypt for its password encryption. It is one of the strongest encryption methods commonly used for passwords.

To use Bcrypt inside Masonite, you have access to a really helpful `password` helper:

```
>>> from masonite.helpers import password
>>> password('secret')
'$2b$12$DFBQYaF6SFZZAcAp.0tN3uWHc5ngCtqZsov3TkIt30Q91Utcf9RAW'
```

You are now free to store that password in your database and use Masonite's authentication classes to verify it.

Cookies

Cookies are also another point of encryption. By default, Masonite even encrypts all cookies generated by your application. This prevents any malicious user from even seeing the values of your cookies. If a JavaScipt package you downloaded happened to have access to your cookies (which it does not, more on that later), we would still be ok because they would get an ecrypted version of your cookies and could do nothing with them.

The reason JavaScript cannot access our cookies is because we set an HTTPOnly flag on the cookie which means our cookies can only be read via HTTP requests. In other words, only our application and server should be able to read them. This is another security point. Just because your code doesn't have any vulnerabilities does not mean any of the 1000 packages you might download from the Node Package Manager will not. Any JavaScript code (or any code, really) that you introduce to your application could be a point of attack for a malicious actor.

Signing on Your Own

You can even sign your own code if you wanted exactly like how Masonite does it.

By default the KEY environment variable is used to do the signing:

```
from masonite.auth import Sign

sign = Sign()
signed = sign.sign('value') # PSJDUudbs87SB....
sign.unsign(signed) # 'value'
```

Under the hood, Masonite calls this class. If you needed to sign things yourself such as user supplied information, you could. It could be a great advertising mark if you could say that not even you can see the users' information.

Once a value is encrypted, it MUST be decrypted using the same secret key that encrypted it. If some values are being signed with a secret key that is revoked, then you may not decrypt values using a new secret key. The value will be forever encrypted until the secret key that was used to encrypt it is then used to decrypt it.

Keep this in mind when signing values and then your secret key is leaked. You will need to change your secret key but all signed strings will never e able to be unsigned.

## CHAPTER 7

Authentication

In the last few chapters, we've learned a lot about creating forms and using them to populate a database. One thing that's quite common for web applications is trying this kind of data to a user account.

You probably got a ton of different "user accounts" for the services you use. Maybe you're on Twitter or Facebook. These connect the data you post, and the things you like to see, to a personalized "identity."

Masonite offers a lot of tooling in this area, so that we don't have to do the heavy lifting every time we build one of these user registration systems. So, in this chapter, we're going to learn about how to use this tooling.

How do I Authenticate Users?

It may surprise you to know that we're already using all the different bits we need to authenticate users. To be clear, there are many different kinds of authentication.

The kind we're going to learn about compares user credentials to database records and remembers the presence of valid credentials so the user can move about where unauthenticated users would otherwise not be able to.

To that end, we'll see how Masonite helps us set up secure forms for accepting those credentials. We'll look at some of the code that compares the credentials to those in the database and tells us whether or not the user credentials are valid.

Finally, we'll see how a successful login is "remembered" and can also be used in conjunction with other database records.

Using the Tools Provided

This code can be found at `https://github.com/assertchris/friday-server/tree/chapter-8`.

© Christopher Pitt and Joe Mancuso 2020
C. Pitt and J. Mancuso, *The Definitive Guide to Masonite*, https://doi.org/10.1007/978-1-4842-5602-2_7

The very first thing we need to do is use a craft command to generate some new auth-related files:

```
craft auth
```

This does quite a bit, so let's look at each piece on its own. First, it creates a bunch of new routes. We can see them just after the routes we've already defined:

```
ROUTES = ROUTES + [
    Get().route('/login', 'LoginController@show').name('login'),
    Get().route('/logout', 'LoginController@logout').name('logout'),
    Post().route('/login', 'LoginController@store'),
    Get().route('/register', 'RegisterController@show').name('register'),
    Post().route('/register', 'RegisterController@store'),
    # Get().route('/home', 'HomeController@show').name('home'),
    Get().route('/email/verify',
'ConfirmController@verify_show').name('verify'),
    Get().route('/email/verify/send', 'ConfirmController@send_verify_
    email'),
    Get().route('/email/verify/@id:signed', 'ConfirmController@confirm_
    email'),
    Get().route('/password', 'PasswordController@forget').name('forgot.
    password'),
    Post().route('/password', 'PasswordController@send'),
    Get().route('/password/@token/reset', 'PasswordController@reset').
    name('password.reset'),
    Post().route('/password/@token/reset', 'PasswordController@update'),
]
```

This is from `routes/web.py`.

The way this code is inserted – by using `ROUTES = ROUTES + [...]` – means it won't overwrite existing routes. You may want to change the formatting of how these are added.

For example, you may prefer to put them in a group. That's ok. Just make sure you keep them pointing at the same controllers, and adjust the URLs you call accordingly.

The next thing the `auth` command does is generate those controllers. The main ones are `RegisterController` and `LoginController`, main in the sense that most of the "authentication" work is done in them. `RegisterController` provides actions for showing the registration form and persisting the user accounts.

`LoginController` provides actions for showing the login form and for checking the credentials against database records.

It's curious that the "check these credentials" method is named `store`, but that's probably to be consistent with other actions which are intended to be used with POST requests.

The other controllers are used for password resets and email verification – great functionality to have built in, but entirely optional.

Feel free to rename these controllers and their actions, to make them more understandable to you. Just remember to update the associated routes, so everything keeps working.

The third change is the views which `auth` adds. They're all put in the `resources/templates/auth` folder and correspond with the actions in the new controllers. Take some time to look through the controllers and templates, to get a feel for how they're put together.

Wait, Haven't I Seen "User" Things Already?

You may have noticed some user-related files, in the codebase, already, specifically the `User` model and the `CreateUsersTable` migration. These exist in all new Masonite installations, in part because the auth configuration also does (and depends on the model, which depends on the existence of the migration).

It's a strange dependency chain, but all it means is that fresh applications include a small piece of the puzzle, and the rest of the pieces come from `craft auth`.

Before we can use the register and login forms, we need to make sure everything is migrated:

```
craft migrate:refresh --seed
```

If you encounter errors, here, remember you need to have a MySQL driver installed (using `pip install mysqlclient`) and to configure the correct database details in `.env`.

You should now see a `users` table, which is where the `User` model will get and put its data. Let's create a new account, by running `craft serve` and going to the registration page, as shown in Figure 7-1.

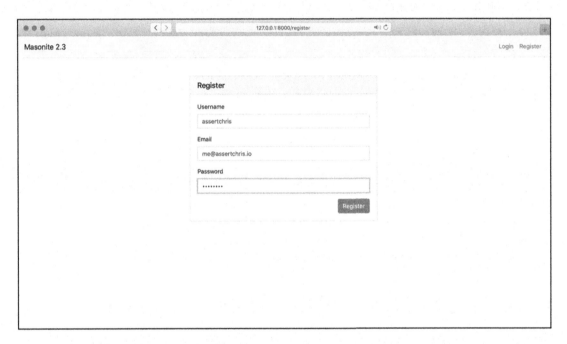

Figure 7-1. *Creating new users*

That should automatically log us in, but in case it doesn't (or you want to log in later on), we can go to the `/login` page (Figure 7-2) and use the same credentials there.

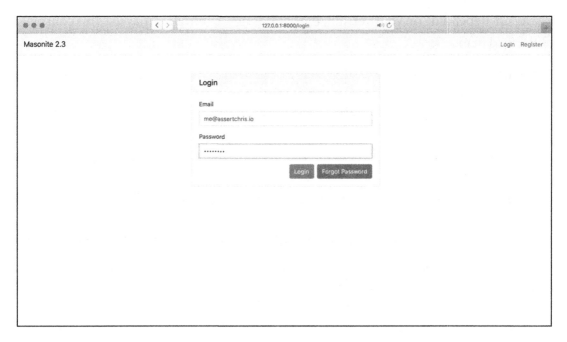

Figure 7-2. *Logging in*

Notice how there's a new record in the users table. That's you!

How Do I Use Different Fields?

By default, the email field is used to identify users. That's the name of the field which will be used in the login method:

```
auth.login(request.input('email'), request.input('password'))
```

This is from app/http/controllers/LoginController.py.

Depending on the version of Masonite you're using, your model may have a constant defined for this:

```
__auth__ = 'email'
```

This is from app/User.py.

127

Again, depending on your version, the various new controllers may use this constant as the field name:

```
auth.login(
    request.input(auth_config.AUTH['model']. __auth__),
    request.input('password')
)
```

This is from app/http/controllers/RegisterController.py.

I prefer all references to use the same, so if I see multiple variations, then I'll change them all to use the constant or to use a hard-coded value. I recommend you do the same, so the code is more understandable.

In any case, this is how Masonite compares login credentials to existing database records. It also means we can exchange "email" for another field. The core authentication code references the constant, so we can change that:

```
__auth__ = 'name'
```

This is from app/User.py.

```
if auth.login(
    request.input(auth_config.AUTH['model']. __auth__),
    request.input('password')
):

    return request.redirect('/home')
```

This is from app/http/controllers/LoginController.py.

If you're going to change this field, I recommend you make whatever field you switch to a unique field. You can do this at a migration level and at a validation level.

How Do I Log the User in Automatically?

RegisterController is a good example of logging the user in automatically, but it's not the only way. Say we know who the user is, but we don't have their login credentials on hand. In that case, we can log them in by their ID:

```
auth.login_by_id(user.id)
```

Turns out, there might be occasions where you have the user (and their ID), and they need to do something that requires authentication, but you don't want them to stay logged in.

The auth object also has a once method, which logs the user in without "remembering" that they're logged in, in subsequent requests:

```
auth.once().login_by_id(user.id)

# ...or

auth.once().login(
    request.input('email'),
    request.input('password')
)
```

Logging the User Out

While we're on the topic of logging the user in, it's also useful to know that the user can be logged out with another method:

```
def logout(self, request: Request, auth: Auth):
    auth.logout()
    return request.redirect('/login')
```

This is from app/http/controllers/LoginController.py.

Using Tokens (JWT) Instead of Credentials

Masonite ships with different ways of authenticating. Our application only really needs credential authentication, but it's useful to know that JWT (token-based) authentication is also supported.

Check out the official documentation to learn more about configuring it: `https://docs.masoniteproject.com/security/authentication#jwt-driver`.

How Do I Protect Parts of My App?

Logging users in to your application goes hand in hand with protecting parts of it from being seen and/or used by users who aren't logged in. Let's look at a couple ways to "secure" parts of our application.

The first way was introduced to us when we ran the `craft auth` command. Look at `HomeController`:

```python
def show(self, request: Request, view: View, auth: Auth):
    if not auth.user():
        request.redirect('/login')

    return view.render('home', {
        'name':
            request.param('name') or request.input('name'),
    })
```

This is from `app/http/controllers/HomeController.py`.

When we're curious about whether or not a user is logged in, we can introduce the `auth: Auth` object into our actions. `auth().user()` will either be empty or it will have a `User` model object, associated with the currently logged in user.

This is effective, but I guess it can lead to a lot of repetition. Additionally, we might forget to add this to all the actions that require it. I find it a lot easier to decide whether an action should be "protected" when I define the route:

```
RouteGroup(
    [
        Match(['GET', 'POST'], '/@name', 'HomeController@show').name('with-
        name'),
Match(['GET', 'POST'], '/', 'HomeController@show').name('without-name'),
    ],
    prefix='/home',
    name='home-',
    middleware=['auth'],
),
```

This is from `routes/web.py`.

We can organize protected routes in route groups and define a `middleware` argument for the whole group. The `auth` middleware is built into Masonite, so we don't have to define it ourselves.

We haven't spent a lot of time learning about Middleware, but it's the subject of the next chapter, so we'll dive in then.

Alternatively, we can secure individual routes:

```
Match(['GET', 'POST'], '/home', 'HomeController@show')
    .name('without-name')
    .middleware('auth'),
```

This is from `routes/web.py`.

Both of these approaches (named argument and `middleware` method) accept a list of middleware or a single middleware string. It's up to you whether you want to take the declarative approach, of protecting routes, or the imperative approach, of protected actions inside themselves.

How Do I Ensure Valid Emails?

I want us to end this chapter by taking a brief look at email verification. I don't want to go too deep into the mechanics, because I feel the code Masonite has automatically generated is amazing for most situations.

When we're looking for "valid" email addresses from our users, there's only one effective solution. Sure, we can use form validation to say whether or not an email address *looks* valid, but the only effective way to know whether it *is* valid is to send email to it.

That's the purpose of email verification. It's a way to make sure a user's email address is the one they say it is, so we can communicate effectively with them going forward.

To that end, the CreateUsersTable migration includes a timestamp called verified_ at, and the auth command generates routes and controllers and views to allow users to verify their email addresses.

To enable it, we need to change the default User model:

```
from config.database import Model
from masonite.auth import MustVerifyEmail

class User(Model, MustVerifyEmail):
    __fillable__ = ['name', 'email', 'password']
    __auth__ = 'email'
```

This is from app/User.py.

In addition, we need to introduce a new kind of middleware, which will promote the user to verify their email address:

```
RouteGroup(
        [
            Match(['GET', 'POST'], '/@name', 'HomeController@show').
            name('with- name'),
        ],
        prefix='/home',
        name='home-',
        middleware=['auth', 'verified'],
    ),
```

```
Match(['GET', 'POST'], '/home', 'HomeController@show')
    .name('without-name')
    .middleware('auth', 'verified'),
```

This is from `routes/web.py`.

Now, when the user's `verified_at` field is empty, they'll be prompted to verify their email address, even if they've logged in already, as shown in Figure 7-3.

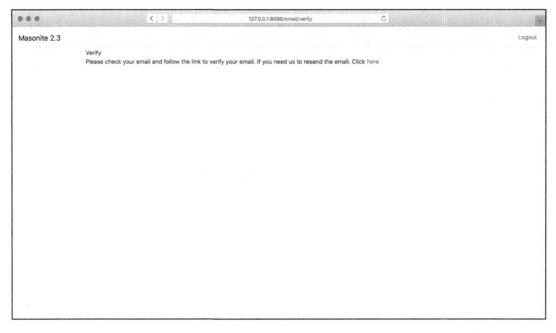

Figure 7-3. *Prompting for email verification*

You might need to configure how Masonite sends email, before you'll see these verification emails: `https://docs.masoniteproject.com/useful-features/mail#configuring-drivers`. We'll dig into this configuration when we add notifications to our app, in Chapter 11.

Summary

In this chapter, we learned about the authentication tooling Masonite provides, how to use it, and how to customize the experience to suit our application.

It's powerful stuff, and you'll undoubtedly need to use it in a few applications you're likely to build. Best get to grips with it now!

In the next chapter, we're going to take deeper look at middleware. We'll learn how it is, how much of it comes with a new application, and how to make our own.

## CHAPTER 8

Creating Middleware

So now that we know what middleware is, let's walk through how middleware is created.

Let's create a middleware and then talk about each section of the middleware. We'll keep this simple for now and just create a simple Hello World middleware and talk through it. Then we'll get into the more complex middleware for our specific application.

If you haven't yet caught on, we will be using a craft command for this:

```
$ craft middleware HelloWorld
```

This will create a `HelloWorldMiddleware.py` file for you inside the `app/http/middleware` directory.

There is nothing special about this directory, so you can move your middleware out of this directory if you like. Just make sure any imports in your `config/middleware.py` file point to the new location. This is more background information, so don't feel like you need to move them though; this directory is fine.

Constructing Middleware

If we look at this class, you can tell that middleware is an extremely simple class with three parts. Let's go through each part so we know what each is doing and what can be done with it.

It's important to note as well that HTTP middleware and route middleware are constructed exactly the same. The only thing that makes it an HTTP or route middleware is how we register it with Masonite, which we will talk about in an upcoming section.

Initializer

```
class HelloWorldMiddleware:

    def __init__(self, request: Request):
        self.request = request

    # ...
```

© Christopher Pitt and Joe Mancuso 2020
C. Pitt and J. Mancuso, *The Definitive Guide to Masonite*, https://doi.org/10.1007/978-1-4842-5602-2_8

The initializer is a simple __init__ method like any other class. The only thing special about it is that it is resolved by the container. So you can type hint application dependencies in your __init__ method, which will resolve classes much like your controller methods.

Since a lot of middleware requires the request class, Masonite will type hint the request class for you. If your specific middleware doesn't need it, then you can remove it without issues.

The before Method

```
class HelloWorldMiddleware:

    #...

    def before(self):
        print("Hello World")
```

The before method is another simple method. Any code in this method will be responsible for running before the controller method is called. In the built-in auth middleware, this is what method is used to check if the user is authenticated and tells the request class to redirect back.

This method can also accept variables that we can pass in from our routes file. We will talk about this later on in the chapter.

The **after** Method

```
class HelloWorldMiddleware:
    #...
    def after(self):
        print('Goodbye World')
```

The after method is very similar to the before method except the code is ran after the controller method is called. This is where the logic would go if we wanted to minify the HTML response as an example.

This method can also accept variables that we can pass in from our routes file. We will talk about this later on in the chapter.

Registering Middleware

Now that we created our middleware class, we can register it with Masonite. We can import it into our `config/middleware.py` file and put it into one of two lists. We can put it in the `HTTP_MIDDLEWARE` list or the `ROUTE_MIDDLEWARE` dictionary.

HTTP Middleware

Remember earlier we said that both middleware are constructed the same, so if you want the middleware to run on every request, put it in the `HTTP_MIDDLEWARE` class.

This would look something like

```
from app.http.middleware.HelloWorldMiddleware import
HelloWorldMiddleware

HTTP_MIDDLEWARE = [
    LoadUserMiddleware,
    CsrfMiddleware,
    ResponseMiddleware,
    MaintenanceModeMiddleware,
    HelloWorldMiddleware, # New Middleware
]
```

Notice HTTP middleware is just a list, so you can just append it to the list. The order of your middleware may not matter, but it actually might.

The order the middleware is run is the same order you put it in the list. So the `LoadUserMiddleware` will run first and then the `HelloWorldMiddleware` will run last. Since our `HelloWorldMiddleware` just prints some text to the terminal, we can add it to the bottom of the list since it doesn't really depend on anything.

On the other hand, if the middleware relied on the user, then we should make sure our middleware is after the `LoadUserMiddleware`. This way the user is loaded into the request class and then our middleware has access to it. As you can tell, the `LoadUserMiddleware` is first for exactly that reason.

Now the HTTP middleware is fully registered with Masonite and it will now run on every request. In a bit, we will see what the output will look like. Before we do that, we'll talk about how to register route middleware.

Route Middleware

Now route middleware again is the same as HTTP middleware, but registering it is a bit different. Right off the bat we can notice that the route middleware is a dictionary. This means we need to bind it to some key.

This key is what we will use to attach the middleware to our routes. We want to name this middleware something short and sweet. We can use the key helloworld as the key and make the middleware the value in the dictionary. This will look something like

```
from app.http.middleware.HelloWorldMiddleware import
HelloWorldMiddleware

ROUTE_MIDDLEWARE = {
    'auth':  AuthenticationMiddleware,
    'verified': VerifyEmailMiddleware,
    'helloworld': HelloWorldMiddleware,
}
```

The naming convention is up to you, but I like to try to keep it to one word. If you need to split into more than one word, we can name it something like hello.world or hello-world. Just be sure not to use the : character since Masonite will splice on that key in our routes file. You'll see more of what that means in the route section in a little bit.

Using the Middleware

So we have talked about what to use middleware for, the different types of middleware we can create, how to create both of those middleware, and finally how to register both of them with Masonite.

Now we will finally get to how we can use the middleware we created. Now the HTTP middleware, which is the one we put inside the list, is already ready to go. We don't actually have to do anything further.

If we start navigating our application and open our terminal, then we may see something that looks like

```
hello world
INFO:root:"GET /login HTTP/1.1" 200 10931
goodbye world
```

```
hello world
INFO:root:"GET /register HTTP/1.1" 200 12541
goodbye world
```

```
hello world
INFO:root:"GET /dashboard HTTP/1.1" 200 4728
goodbye world
```

Notice we start seeing the hello world and goodbye world print statements before and after our controller methods are hit.

Route middleware on the other hand is a bit different. We will need to use this middleware by specifying the key in our routes file.

For example, if we want to use the helloworld middleware we made earlier, we can add it to a route that looks something like

```
Get('/dashboard', 'YourController@show').middleware('helloworld')
```

This will now run the middleware ONLY for this route and not for any other routes.

Looking back to our previous terminal output, our new application will look something like this:

```
INFO:root:"GET /login HTTP/1.1" 200 10931
INFO:root:"GET /register HTTP/1.1" 200 12541
```

```
hello world
INFO:root:"GET /dashboard HTTP/1.1" 200 4728
goodbye world
```

Notice we only put the middleware on the /dashboard route, so therefore it will only be executed for that specific route:

```
Get('/dashboard',
'YourController@show').middleware('helloworld:Hello,Joe')
```

Remember before we say to make sure your middleware aliases don't have a : in the name because Masonite will splice on that? Well this is what that meant. Masonite will splice on the : character and pass all variables after it to the middleware.

Now that we said we are passing these values to the middleware, let's look at what the middleware will look like:

```
class HelloWorldMiddleware:

    #...

    def before(*self*, *greeting*, *name*):
        pass

    def before(*self*, *greeting*, *name*):
        pass
```

Whatever we pass into the route, BOTH the `before` and `after` middleware need those two parameters.

As you might have guessed, the parameters are in the same order as you specify them in the routes. So `greeting` will be `Hello` and `name` will be `Joe`.

Middleware Stacks

Middleware stacks are another simple concept. There will be times when some of your routes look very repetitive with the same middleware over and over again. We can group middleware into middleware "stacks," or lists of middleware, in order to run all those middleware under one alias.

For example, let's say we have some middleware that we want to run all under a single alias. Just so we can use a better example, we may see ourselves using very similar middleware over and over again:

```
ROUTES = [
(Get('/dashboard', 'YourController@show')
    .middleware('auth', 'trim', 'admin')),

(Get('/dashboard/user', 'YourController@show')
    .middleware('auth', 'trim', 'admin')),
]
```

Notice the middleware seems a bit repetitive. What we can do here is create a middleware stack to group them. This looks like

```
ROUTE_MIDDLEWARE = {
    'auth':  AuthenticationMiddleware,
    'verified': VerifyEmailMiddleware,
    'dashboard': [
        AuthenticationMiddleware,
        TrimStringsMiddleware,
        AdminMiddleware,
    ]
}
```

We can then refactor our routes a bit to use this stack:

```
ROUTES = [
(Get('/dashboard',  'YourController@show')
    .middleware('dashboard')),

(Get('/dashboard/user',   'YourController@show')
    .middleware('dashboard')),
]
```

CHAPTER 9

Using Helpers

We've already covered a lot of ground, so we're going to change gears and talk about helpers. In short, helpers are functions we can use from anywhere that do things for us quicker or more efficiently than we could otherwise do. It's tricky to explain their use without looking at code, so that's what we're going to do.

These helpers are available, globally, so you won't need to import most of them. I'll tell you what the exceptions are, when it's important.

The Request and Auth Helpers

This code can be found at `https://github.com/assertchris/friday-server/tree/chapter-10`.

We're no stranger to the Request class. It's common for us to inject it into a controller action:

```
def show(self, request: Request, view: View):
    return view.render('home', {
        'name': request.param('name'),
    })
```

What if we wanted to use the request from somewhere else? I'm not talking about whether we should, or not, but rather, "could we?"

An obvious place we might want to use it would be in the view:

```
@extends 'layout.html'
```

© Christopher Pitt and Joe Mancuso 2020

C. Pitt and J. Mancuso, *The Definitive Guide to Masonite*, https://doi.org/10.1007/978-1-4842-5602-2_9

```
@block content
    hello {{ request().param('name') }}
@endblock
```

If you like this style, you may like using the request helper in actions, as well:

```
from masonite.auth import Auth
from masonite.view import View

class HomeController:
    def show(self, view: View, auth: Auth):
        return view.render('home', {
            'name': request().param('name') or request().input('name'),
        })
```

Similarly, we can shorten the auth code by using an Auth helper:

```
from masonite.view import View

class HomeController:
    def show(self, view: View):
        return view.render('home', {
            'name': request().param('name') or auth().email,
        })
```

This is from app/http/controllers/HomeController.py.

The auth() function can be super helpful, but be careful using it. If the user isn't logged in, then auth() will return False. Your code should take that into account. It's also great in the view layer:

```
<!doctype html>
<html lang="en">
    <head>
        <meta charset="utf-8">
        <link href="/static/style.css" rel="stylesheet" type="text/css">
    </head>
```

```
<body>
    <div class="container mx-auto p-4">
        @if (auth())
            <a href="{{ route('logout') }}">log out</a>
        @else
            <a href="{{ route('login') }}">log in</a>
        @endif
        @block content
            <!-- template content will be put here-->
        @endblock
    </div>
</body>
</html>
```

This is from `resources/templates/layout.html`.

The auth() function will return None if the user isn't logged in, which can be reused to toggle UI based on the presence of a user session. This is also an example of another helper.

The Route Helper

The Route helper is essential for larger apps, but you have to name your routes for it to work:

```
Get('/profile/@id', 'ProfileController@show').name('profile')
```

We can use the route() function to build out any named route, including routes that we've defined parameters for:

```
<a href="{{ route('profile', { 'id': auth().id }) }}">public profile</a>
```

The Container and Resolve Helpers

Sometimes we may want to add our own classes and functions to the service container, we learned about in Chapter 4. You may not always be inside an action with access to "the app," but you can access the container helper:

```
from app.Service import Service
container().bind('Service', Service)

# ...later

container().make('Service')
```

Service is an example, here. Think of it as a placeholder for whatever custom class your next application may need.

This is great for extending things already in the container and for accessing things stored in the container from other contexts, like views and models. In a similar vein, it can be useful to resolve dependencies of a function, like Masonite does automatically for actions.

Here's an example of how a controller action's request parameter is automatically resolved:

```
from masonite.helpers import compact

# ...later

def respond(request: Request):
    action = request.param('action')
    name = request.param('name')

    if (action == 'read'):
        return view('read.html', compact(name))

    if (action == 'write'):
        return view('write.html', compact(name))

def handle(self):
    return resolve(respond)
```

The resolve helper takes another function and resolves the parameters it needs out of the container. This is also an example of our first non-global helper (the `compact()` function), which takes a list of variables and returns a dictionary where each key is the string variable name and each value is the variable's value.

Non-global helpers are just helpers you still need to import in every file where they are used. Here, we're importing the compact helper. You can make non-global helpers globally available by following a similar pattern to this: `https://docs.masoniteproject.com/the-basics/helper-functions#introduction`.

The Env and Config Helpers

`env()` and `config()` are closely related helpers, which pull configuration variables out of the environment (or `.env` files) and files within the `config` folder, respectively. The main difference between them, other than that they look in different files, is that data returned from `env()` is aggressively cached, whereas data returned from `config()` can be changed and lazy-loaded.

When using these, it's best to only use `env()` inside config files and only use `config()` everywhere else:

```
FROM = {
    'address': env('MAIL_FROM_ADDRESS', 'hello@example.com'),
    'name': env('MAIL_FROM_NAME', 'Masonite')
}
```

This is from `config/mail.py`.

As this demonstrates, the second parameter to the `env()` function is a default value. This is great if or when the environment variable isn't guaranteed to exist. Once the configuration variables are in a config file, we can pull them out with the `config()` function:

```
from config import mail as mail_config

# ...later

print(mail_config.FROM['address'])
```

The Dump-and-Die Helper

Like so much of Masonite, the dump-and-die helper is inspired by the same helper in Laravel: `https://laravel.com/docs/6.x/helpers#method-dd`. It's a quick way to stop what's going on, so you can inspect the contents of multiple variables:

```
dd(User.find(1).email, request().params('email'))
```

It's not a step debugger, but it's great in a pinch!

Summary

In this chapter, we've taken a look at the most popular helper functions. They're certainly not the only helper functions, so I encourage you to take a look at the documentation to learn more: `https://docs.masoniteproject.com/the-basics/helper-functions`. Chances are you'll find something there that you like.

In the next chapter, we're going to learn about all the different ways we can send notifications from our applications.

## CHAPTER 10

Doing Work in the Background

In the previous chapter, we looked at all sorts of ways to make and send notifications. It's an invaluable tool for large applications and more so for applications that need to perform tasks in the background.

Think of the web sites you use regularly, sites like YouTube, Facebook, Twitter, and Google. You know what they have in common (apart from a lot of money)? They all need to do boring work outside of the request/response cycle.

YouTube transforms videos from one format to many different formats. Facebook and Twitter crunch user data and send notifications to your friends and family, even when they're not online. Google crawls the whole Internet, with an army of hungry robots.

If these sites suddenly lost the ability to do work when nobody else was looking, they'd stop working altogether. And, odds are you're going to build something that needs to do similar work in the background.

How Do I Speed Up My Application with Queues?

Queues are the main tool Masonite provides, for pushing work into the background. A queue is a stand-alone program, which runs on a server. It could be on the same server as the Masonite app, but that's not a requirement.

This is how applications interact with queues:

1. The application needs to do some work. In our case, it's work that should be done outside of the request/response cycle.

2. The application connects to the queue and sends a summary of the work that needs to be done to the queue.

© Christopher Pitt and Joe Mancuso 2020
C. Pitt and J. Mancuso, *The Definitive Guide to Masonite*, https://doi.org/10.1007/978-1-4842-5602-2_10

3. The same application (or another, it doesn't really matter which) connects to the same queue and checks if any new "jobs" have been added to it.

4. If that "worker" script gets new jobs, it takes those jobs off the queue, does them, and deletes them from the queue.

5. If an error occurs, the job could remain on the queue or it could be deleted or it could expire. All depends on configuration.

So, in essence, we can speed up our application by taking *work that doesn't need to be done immediately* and send it to be processed by a queue worker.

Using YouTube as an example:

1. A creator uploads a video to YouTube. There's a bit of background processing that happens, but all the user sees is a details form and a progress indicator. They can still use the form and do other things on the site. Once the original video is uploaded, they don't even need to stay on the site for the rest of the processing to happen.

2. YouTube sends the original video to a queue, and the first "job" is to create a low-quality version of it, quickly. This ensures there's something for viewers to watch as quickly as possible, while higher-quality versions are created.

3. YouTube emails the creator the moment the low-quality version is created and ready to be viewed. This happens at the end of the "job" process, regardless of whether or not the creator still has YouTube open.

4. Higher-quality versions of the original video are created, and as they become available, new quality options appear in the video player.

There are many queued operations at play. Without them, the creator would need to leave the YouTube tab open for hours, or risk the video not uploading and processing correctly. Viewers would need to wait longer than necessary. Emails wouldn't get sent.

When and Where Do I Use Queueing?

You should use job queues wherever you need to do large tasks. If you need to adjust request timeout configuration, that's a task that should be done in a queue. If closing the tab leads to avoidable loss of data and/or processing, that's a task that should be done in a queue.

If the tasks are small, but nonessential or non-immediate, consider putting those in a queue. If you need to send emails or archive files on the server or export user data, those can be done in queues.

Finding Files to Cache

This code can be found at `https://github.com/assertchris/friday-server/tree/chapter-12`.

Let's continue with an example in our home personal assistant. We've already got a way to search for podcasts we like to listen to, in the home. Now, let's look at how we might work with them.

First off, we need to connect the podcast search results to the subscriptions work we did:

```
<form action="{{ route('podcasts-subscribe') }}" method="POST">
    {{ csrf_field }}
    {{ request_method('POST') }}
    <input type="hidden" name="url" value="{{ podcast.feedUrl }}">
    <input type="hidden" name="title" value="{{ podcast.collectionName }}">
    <button onclick="event.preventDefault(); this.form.
    submit()">subscribe</button>
</form>
```

This is from `resources/templates/podcasts/_podcast.html`.

This button resembles the ones we added on the subscriptions list page. We don't have that controller action, yet, so we need to add it along with a new route:

```python
def do_subscribe(self, request: Request):
    Subscription.create({
        'url': request.input('url'),
        'title': request.input('title'),
        'favorite': False,
    })

    return request.redirect_to('podcasts-show-subscriptions')
```

This is from app/http/controllers/PodcastController.py.

```python
Post('/subscribe', 'PodcastController@do_subscribe').name('-subscribe'),
```

This is from routes/web.py.

A Post request is the best request method for this, in semantic terms. We're creating a whole new record, as opposed to updating or deleting existing records.

We, therefore, put the title and url values in hidden fields and extract them from the request with request.input. Following the successful subscription, we can redirect to the list of subscriptions.

Let's expand the subscriptions page, to show the five most recent episodes per podcast:

```python
def show_subscriptions(self, view: View):
    favorites = Subscription.where('favorite', True).get()
    subscriptions = Subscription.where('favorite', '!=', True).get()

    self.get_episodes(favorites)
    self.get_episodes(subscriptions)

    return view.render('podcasts.subscriptions', {
        'favorites': favorites,
        'subscriptions': subscriptions,
    })
```

```python
def get_episodes(self, podcasts):
    for podcast in podcasts:
        podcast.episodes = []

        for entry in feedparser.parse(podcast.url).entries:
            enclosure = next(
                link for link in entry.links if link.rel == 'enclosure'
            )

            if (enclosure):
                podcast.episodes.append({
                    'title': entry.title,
                    'enclosure': enclosure,
                })
```

This is from app/http/controllers/PodcastController.py.

We added the feedparser library some time ago. Now, we're going to use it to find the media files for each podcast episode. We do this by defining a get_episodes method, which crawls through the entries in a list of podcasts.

In each entry, we look for the link with the enclosure type and add it back to the

```html
<ol class="list-decimal">
    @for episode in subscription.episodes[:5]
        <li>{{ episode.title }}</li>
    @endfor
</ol>
```

This is from resources/templates/podcasts/_subscription.html.

Creating Jobs

Now that we have files to download, it's time to make our first Job class:

```
craft job DownloadEpisode
```

This creates a new file, which resembles

```
from masonite.queues import Queueable

class DownloadEpisode(Queueable):
    def __init__(self):
        pass

    def handle(self):
        pass
```

This is from app/jobs/DownloadEpisode.py.

Jobs are just classes that are passed through a queue. Let's print a couple things in this one and trigger it from a new controller action.

```
def __init__(self):
    print("in __init__ method")

def handle(self):
    print("in handle method")
```

This is from app/jobs/DownloadEpisode.py.

```
Post('/download', 'PodcastController@do_download').name('-download'),
```

This is from routes/web.py.

```
from app.jobs.DownloadEpisode import DownloadEpisode
from masonite import Queue

# ...later
```

```
def do_download(self, request: Request, queue: Queue):
    queue.push(DownloadEpisode)
    return "done"
```

This is from app/http/controllers/PodcastController.py.

```
<ol class="list-decimal">
    @for episode in subscription.episodes[:5]
        <li>
            {{ episode.title }}
            <form action="{{ route('podcasts-download') }}" method="POST">
                {{ csrf_field }}
                {{ request_method('POST') }}
                <input type="hidden" name="url" value="{{ episode.
                 enclosure.href }}">
                <button onclick="event.preventDefault(); this.form.
                 submit()">download</button>
            </form>
        </li>
    @endfor
</ol>
```

This is from resources/templates/podcasts/_subscription.html.

As we click this "download" button (on the /podcasts route), we should see a few new things happening:

1. The browser should show a mostly blank page, with "done."

2. The terminal window (in which the craft serve is running) should show in _init_method.

This means we're successfully putting the `DownloadEpisode` job into the queue, but the missing in handle method method shows us that the job is not yet being picked up.

That's because the default queue configuration makes the jobs run in the background:

```
# ...
DRIVERS = {
    'async': {
        'mode': 'threading'
    },
    # ...
}
```

This is from `config/queue.py`.

The jobs are being executed, but they're being executed in other threads, so we can't see that they are being handled or printing. We can configure the async queue to block execution of the jobs, so they'll be executed immediately:

```
# ...

DRIVERS = {
    'async': {
        'mode': 'threading',
        'blocking': env('APP_DEBUG')
    },
    # ...
}
```

This is from `config/queue.py`.

Here, we're telling Masonite to make the jobs execute immediately, but only when the app is in debug mode. If we click the "download" button again, we should see the job is being executed. We still don't see the printed output, but at least we know it's happening, now.

Downloading Files

Let's start downloading the podcast episodes. We can do this in the handle method, but we'll need the URL:

```
def do_download(self, request: Request, queue: Queue):
    url = request.input('url')
    folder = 'storage/episodes'

    queue.push(DownloadEpisode(url, folder))

    return request.redirect_to('podcasts-show-subscriptions')
```

This is from app/http/controllers/PodcastController.py.

Jobs take constructor arguments, just like any other Python class. In this case, we can pass the URL to the podcast episode and the folder in which we want the audio file stored.

It's probably a good idea to redirect back to the subscriptions page – that's a much better experience than just printing the string "done."

Now, we can use some file-fu to store the episode's audio file in the storage/episodes folder.

```
from masonite.queues import Queueable
import base64
import requests

class DownloadEpisode(Queueable):

    def __init__(self, url, folder):
        self.url = url
        self.folder = folder

    def handle(self):
        encodedBytes = base64.b64encode(self.url.encode("utf-8"))
        name = str(encodedBytes, "utf-8")
```

```
response = requests.get(self.url, stream=True)
file = open(self.folder + '/' + name + '.mp3', 'wb')

for chunk in response.iter_content(chunk_size=1024*1024):
    if chunk:
        file.write(chunk)
```

This is from `app/jobs/DownloadEpisode.py`.

First up, we generate a safe name for the file. One way to do this is to base64 encode the URL where we're downloading the file from. Then, we make a request to the URL (using the Requests library) and get back a streamed response.

Streamed responses are great (especially for larger files) because they don't have to be entirely in memory. If we read many large audio files, over many requests, the server might run out of memory to serve new requests. Instead, streamed responses are broken up so that only small parts of the files we download are in memory at a time.

We write each file chunk, as we get it, to the destination file. There are a couple things you might need to do, at this point:

1. Create the `storage/episodes` folder. If you're seeing a `FileNotFoundError` or `NotADirectoryError`, from the job execution (check the terminal), then this is probably the reason.

2. Install the Requests library, if you haven't already done so. `pip install requests` should do the trick.

For the sake of keeping things simple, I am not handling the downloads as well as I could. We should, for instance, be checking that the file is a valid audio file and that we're saving it with the same extension that it already has. In addition, we could create a new model for these downloads, so that we could save the details for later.

If everything's set up correctly, clicking the "Download" button should now redirect us to the do_download action, which should execute the job and redirect us back. If we're running the queue in blocking mode, this means we'll have the audio downloaded by the time we're back at the subscriptions page.

Showing Downloaded Files

Now that we are downloading files, we can show which episodes have been downloaded already:

```python
def get_episodes(self, podcasts):
    for podcast in podcasts:
        podcast.episodes = []

        for entry in feedparser.parse(podcast.url).entries:
            enclosure = next(
                link for link in entry.links if link.rel == 'enclosure'
            )

            if (enclosure):
                encodedBytes = base64.b64encode(
                    enclosure.href.encode("utf-8"))
                name = str(encodedBytes, "utf-8")

                is_downloaded = False

                if path.exists('storage/episodes/' + name + '.mp3'):
                    is_downloaded = True

                podcast.episodes.append({
                    'title': entry.title,
                    'enclosure': enclosure,
                    'is_downloaded': is_downloaded,
                })
```

This is from app/http/controllers/PodcastController.py.

When we find enclosures for episodes, we can check to see if the file has already been downloaded, by checking the base64 encoded name against files in the storage/episodes folder.

Then, we can use this to selectively hide the "Download" button, in the view:

```
@for episode in subscription.episodes[:5]
    <li>
        {{ episode.title }}
        @if episode.is_downloaded != True
            <form action="{{ route('podcasts-download') }}" method="POST">
                {{ csrf_field }}
                {{ request_method('POST') }}
                <input type="hidden" name="url" value="{{ episode.
                 enclosure.href }}">
                <button onclick="event.preventDefault(); this.form.
                 submit()">download</button>
            </form>
        @endif
    </li>
@endfor
```

This is from `resources/templates/podcasts/_subscription.html`.

We could even go so far as to replace the download form with an audio player, since we have the file at our disposal.

Using Different Queue Providers

We've only just used the async provider, but there are a few others we could also try. You should use the provider that suits your server setup and the types of jobs you want to push into it.

AMPQ/RabbitMQ

RabbitMQ (via the AMPQ provider) is a queue application, which runs alongside the Masonite server. It could run on a separate server, just the same, because Masonite connects to it through an IP address and port.

Have you seen these configuration settings, yet?

```
QUEUE_DRIVER=async
QUEUE_USERNAME=
QUEUE_VHOST=
QUEUE_PASSWORD=
QUEUE_HOST=
QUEUE_PORT=
QUEUE_CHANNEL=
```

This is from `.env`.

These control which queue provider is used and, in the case of RabbitMQ, how Masonite connects to them. You cannot use RabbitMQ in the same blocking way we've been using the async provider.

I suggest you do all your local development using the blocking driver and leave RabbitMQ for production.

Database

If you want greater control over how you handle failed jobs, it's best to use the database provider. This provider places details about failed jobs into the database, so long as you create the appropriate tables:

```
craft queue:table -jobs
craft queue:table -failed
craft migrate
```

The first table is where the ready-to-process jobs are stored. The second is where the failed jobs are recorded. This means you can keep an eye on the failed jobs table and investigate any failures.

You can even build an HTML view of those tables, to keep better track of what is and has been processed through the queue.

If you want to use one of these other providers, be sure to check out the official documentation: `https://docs.masoniteproject.com/v/v2.2/useful-features/queues-and-jobs`.

Summary

In this chapter, we learned about why we should be using queues and how to set them up. Queues are immensely useful, and no large application would exist without something like them.

Spend some time putting an audio play into your application, so you can start to listen to your podcasts.

In the next chapter, we're going to look at another form of inter-process communication, this time between the server and the browser. That's right, we're going to tackle web sockets!

## CHAPTER 11

Adding Websockets with Pusher

We've done a lot of server-side work, but now it's time to do some work in the browser. Specifically, I want us to look at how we can "push" new information to the browser, without the user initiating the action (by clicking a button or typing a message).

"Isn't That Ajax?"

When we looked at creating forms, in Chapter 5, we spoke about Ajax and Websockets. To recap, Ajax is a method for sending requests to the server, without loading a new URL in the browser, and updating small parts of the page when the request completes.

This is simplistic definition of Ajax, but it's also the most common use case for it. The page doesn't *have* to update, when the request completes.

Ajax and "normal" form requests are commonly user-initiated actions. Sometimes, web apps can initiate these actions, but the more drastic the results, the less likely the causes are to be automatic.

There are times when it would be useful not to have to wait for a user action. Imagine you wanted to be notified of a new email or tweet, but you didn't want to have to click a button.

You *could* set up a kind of loop, in the browser, to make Ajax requests, but most of the time they wouldn't show any new data. It would be wasted work, which would slow down other similar operations for zero benefit.

© Christopher Pitt and Joe Mancuso 2020
C. Pitt and J. Mancuso, *The Definitive Guide to Masonite*, https://doi.org/10.1007/978-1-4842-5602-2_11

Websockets, on the other hand, are an open connection to the server. The server can, at any time, push new data through the Websocket, without the user initiating the action or the need for needless HTTP requests.

Installing Pusher

This code can be found at `https://github.com/assertchris/friday-server/tree/chapter-13`.

There are many ways to set up Websockets, but my favorite is through a service called Pusher. It's a hosted Websocket service, which allows pushing new events from a server to a browser, without the server directly supporting Websockets.

Let's get started! Go to `https://pusher.com` and click "Sign Up." I prefer to use my GitHub account, so I have fewer accounts to password protect. Once you're signed up, you should be taken to the dashboard, as shown in Figure 11-1.

Figure 11-1. *The Pusher dashboard*

Next, click the "Create new app" button, and you should see a popup that asks for app details. I've selected Vanilla JS as a front-end tech and Python as a back-end tech.

As illustrated in Figure 11-2, I've also entered "Friday" as the app name, and selected a region close to me.

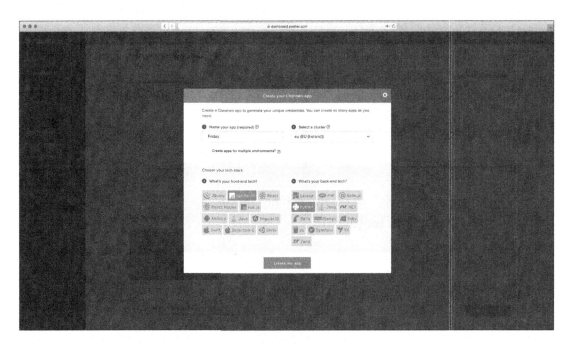

Figure 11-2. *Setting up a new Pusher app*

Integrating Pusher on the Front End

The app page shows the code we'll need to open a connection to pusher. Let's add the front-end code first:

```
<!doctype html>
<html lang="en">
    <head>
        <meta charset="utf-8">
        <link href="/static/style.css" rel="stylesheet" type="text/css">
    </head>
    <body>
        <div class="container mx-auto p-4">
```

```
        @block content
            <!-- template content will be put here-->
        @endblock
    </div>
    <script src="https://js.pusher.com/5.0/pusher.min.js"></script>
    <script>
        Pusher.logToConsole = true;

        var pusher = new Pusher('c158052fb78ff1c7b4b2', {
            cluster: 'eu',
            forceTLS: true
        });

        var channel = pusher.subscribe('my-channel');

        channel.bind('my-event', function(data) {
            console.log(data);
        });
    </script>
    </body>
</html>
```

This is from `resources/templates/layout.html`.

That's a public key, so it's ok for it to be directly in the view, but you may want to consider moving it to the `.env` file. Generally, it's better to put service-related keys (and secrets) in `.env`, and not to commit that file to Git.

Be sure to replace `c158052fb78ff1c7b4b2` with your Pusher application key. I've included mine so you can see exactly where it goes, but it will not work for your application.

Pusher works with the concept of channels. Browsers (or mobile apps, etc.) connect to channels they're interested in, and pusher sends events inside those channels.

Here, we're connecting to the `my-channel` channel and listening for `my-event` events. We'll see those values, again, when we add the server-side code.

Creating Commands

There are a number of places we could trigger Pusher events, but I think it makes sense for us to revisit console commands. Let's install the Pusher library and create a new console command to send messages to all online browsers:

```
pip install pusher
craft command SendMessageToOnlineBrowsers
```

This creates a file resembling:

```
from cleo import Command

class SendMessageToOnlineBrowsersCommand(Command):
    """
    Description of command

    command:name
        {argument : description}
    """

    def handle(self):
        pass
```

This is from app/commands/SendMessageToOnlineBrowsersCommand.py.

Let's customize the command to reflect its purpose and print something:

```
from cleo import Command

class SendMessageToOnlineBrowsersCommand(Command):
    """
    Sends a message to all currently online browsers

    send-messages-to-online-browsers
        {message : The text to send}
    """

    def handle(self):
        print("in the command")
```

This is from app/commands/SendMessageToOnlineBrowsersCommand.py.

Each new console command has a `handle` method, which is called when the console command is invoked. We need to register this command inside `craft`, so let's do that in a new service provider:

`craft provider CraftProvider`

This creates a file resembling:

```
from masonite.provider import ServiceProvider

class CraftProvider(ServiceProvider):
    wsgi = False

    def register(self):
        pass

    def boot(self):
        pass
```

This is from app/providers/CraftProvider.py.

Providers' `register` method is invoked as the app is starting up, whereas the `boot` method is only invoked after the app has fully started up. The distinction is important, because the best place to put services other providers might *want* is in `register`, while the best place to put things that *use* other services is in `boot`.

In this case, we want to make our new `craft` command *available* to other providers and services:

```
from masonite.provider import ServiceProvider
from app.commands.SendMessageToOnlineBrowsers import
SendMessageToOnlineBrowsers

class CraftProvider(ServiceProvider):
    wsgi = False

    def register(self):
```

```
    self.app.bind(
        'SendMessageToOnlineBrowsers',
        SendMessageToOnlineBrowsers()
    )

def boot(self):
    pass
```

This is from app/providers/CraftProvider.py.

This provider, in turn, needs to be registered in the app configuration:

```
from .HttpClientProvider import HttpClientProvider
from .RssParserProvider import RssParserProvider
from .CraftProvider import CraftProvider
```

This is from app/providers/__init__.py.

```
# ...snip

from app.providers import (
    HttpClientProvider,
    RssParserProvider,
    CraftProvider, )

PROVIDERS = [
    # ...snip

    HttpClientProvider,
    RssParserProvider,
    CraftProvider,
]
```

This is from config/providers.py.

Now, when we run the `craft` command, in a new terminal window, we should see the new command we've added, as shown in Figure 11-3.

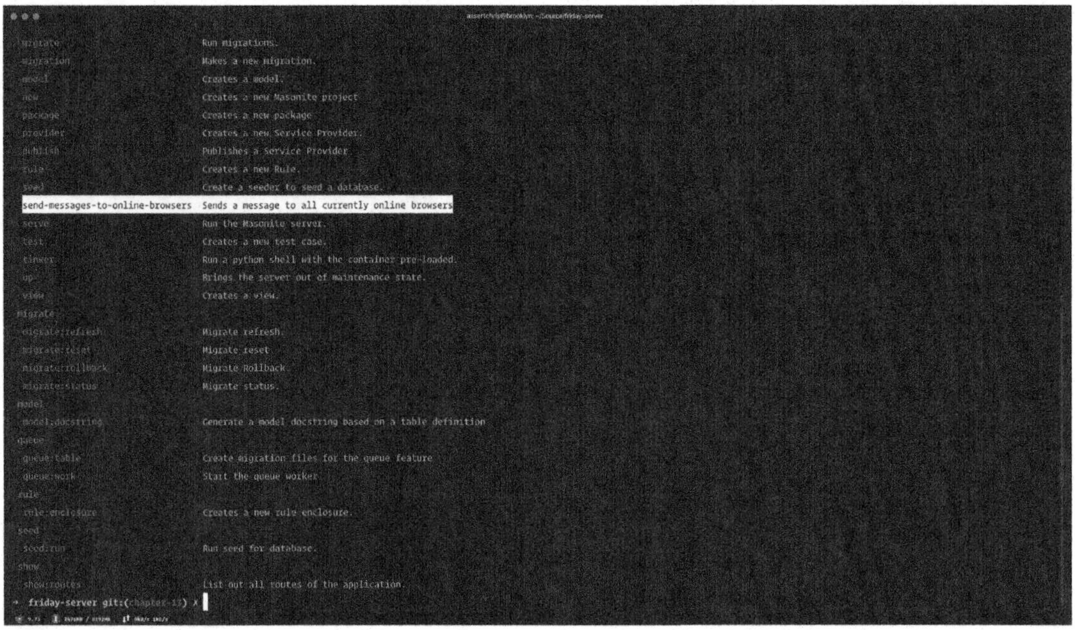

Figure 11-3. *Listing the new command*

And, we can run the command:

```
craft send-messages-to-online-browsers "hello world"
```

Integrating Pusher on the Back End

Ok, so we have a command we can use, but it's not using the message we send through. Let's install the Pusher library and use it in the command:

```
pip install pusher
```

```
from cleo import Command
from pusher import Pusher
```

```python
class SendMessageToOnlineBrowsersCommand(Command):
    """

    Sends a message to all currently online browsers

    send-messages-to-online-browsers
        {message : The text to send}
    """

    def handle(self):
        message = self.argument('message')

        pusher = Pusher(
            app_id='935879',
            key='c158052fb78ff1c7b4b2',
            secret='ab37b95e1648ba5c67cc',
            cluster='eu',
            ssl=True
        )

        pusher.trigger('my-channel', 'my-event', {'message': message})
```

This is from app/commands/SendMessageToOnlineBrowsers.py.

If we run the command, again, we should see the message in the Pusher app window, as demonstrated in Figure 11-4. Remember to use your own Pusher keys, in the layout and command, or this will not work.

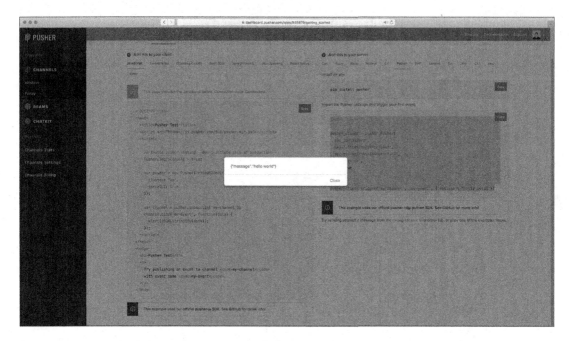

Figure 11-4. *Receiving messages in pusher*

This is super cool. We should see the same events in the JavaScript console, from any page in our app, as shown in Figure 11-5.

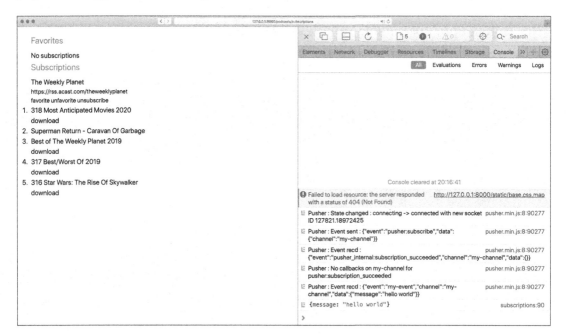

Figure 11-5. *Seeing events in the console*

Acting on Received Messages

Let's add a pop-up window, which shows these messages for a few seconds. We can add the markup in an include and reference it from the JavaScript we already added:

```
<div
    class="
        message
        hidden flex-row items-center justify-center
        absolute top-0 left-0 p-2 m-8
        bg-blue-100 border-2 border-blue-200
    "
>
    <div class="text-blue-700">message text here</div>
    <button class="text-blue-500 ml-2">&cross;</button>
</div>
```

This is from `resources/templates/_message.html`.

```
@include '_message.html' <script src="https://js.pusher.com/5.0/pusher.
min.js"></script>
<script>
    Pusher.logToConsole = true;

    var pusher = new Pusher('c158052fb78ff1c7b4b2', {
        cluster: 'eu',
        forceTLS: true
    });

    var channel = pusher.subscribe('my-channel');
    var message = document.querySelector('.message');
    var messageClose = message.querySelector('button');
    var messageText = message.querySelector('div');

    messageClose.addEventListener('click', function() {
```

```
    message.classList.remove('flex');
    message.classList.add('hidden');
});

channel.bind('my-event', function(data) {
    messageText.innerHTML = data.message;

    message.classList.remove('hidden');
    message.classList.add('flex');

    setTimeout(function() {
        message.classList.remove('flex');
        message.classList.add('hidden');
    }, 1000 * 5 /* 5 seconds */)
});
</script>
```

This is from `resources/templates/layout.html`.

We've customized the JavaScript to look for the message HTML elements and make them visible when a new message comes through. The user can opt to dismiss the message, by clicking the "close" button, or the message will go away by itself.

Summary

In this chapter, we looked at how to install and use Pusher. There are a few other interesting Pusher features, like channel presence and private channels, but they're a bit more involved. Maybe that's a good place to take your Websocket learning further!

Websockets are a powerful tool and one I find myself reaching for often. Think of all the things you *could* tell the user, with a permanently open connection straight to their browser.

CHAPTER 12

Testing

Unit testing is the art of taking small sections of your code (called units) and testing that functionality to ensure that it works properly. For example, you might take a small unit of code, like a controller method, and assert that it returns a view class.

Unit testing is really crucial for any application. There's a lot of frameworks that make unit testing an afterthought, but with Masonite, we wanted to be sure that being able to test your application was absolutely crucial to us.

What Is Integration Testing?

Integration testing is just a broader concept than unit testing. Typically it's a test that touches larger pieces of code or runs through a process similar to what a user would do. For example, you might test that when a user hits an endpoint

- An email gets sent

- A record is added to the database

- A user is redirected to the dashboard

Now unit testing is great, but sometimes testing code in small units doesn't allow you to test things in a larger picture and you could miss out on some key aspects that go untested. So where unit testing falls short, you could do things like integration testing.

We'll go over how to do both of these things in this chapter.

Why Tests in the First Place?

One of the reasons that you should test your application is to ensure that as you're continuously adding new features, old features don't break. I can't tell you the number of times I have changed a small piece of code in one of the requests classes for Masonite and something in some random class broke.

© Christopher Pitt and Joe Mancuso 2020
C. Pitt and J. Mancuso, *The Definitive Guide to Masonite*, https://doi.org/10.1007/978-1-4842-5602-2_12

Before Masonite is released, it will run all tests on the last four major versions of Python. Having automated testing helps make sure that Masonite will run flawlessly on all supported versions of Python.

Now one of the reasons that people don't test their applications is because it does take up a lot of initial time to have to write the tests and it sometimes takes longer to write the whole feature out in addition to the tests. It does take a lot of time to set up a basic test to test the simpler parts of the application. We are usually asserting the same things on different routes. Maybe we assert that a middleware exists on a route or that a user who isn't logged in is not able to access a file.

With Masonite, we took that into account and wanted to make sure that it was as fast as possible to set up these tests. You'll even see why the auto resolving dependency injection aspects of Masonite actually help to test because all of those classes you are type-hinting can all be injected inside your tests. So you can mock a request if your controller takes the request class, then you can just build a new one in your tests and inject it right into your controller method.

Another reason to unit test your application is because there could be an extremely complex business logic rule that needs to always work. For example, having specific items needs to have item restrictions, item sales restrictions. One of these two things failing could mean lawsuits to the business and that's something that you really don't want failing.

Lastly, the reason for unit tests is for refactoring purposes. When refactoring your code, if you have a test behind it, you can ensure that the code worked the same way before you refactored vs. after you're refactoring. These are all reasons to pursue unit testing, and we'll talk about how Masonite handles all of this in a bit before we dive right into creating our tests.

Where Do Our Tests Live?

So before we get into actually creating our tests, it might be good to know where we're actually going to be putting our tests or even how we're going to run them. All tests live in the `tests` directory, and this directory is broken up into a few different directories.

First director is called "`tests/unit`". This is where you'll put all your unit tests.

The next one is "`tests/framework`". This is where you will put all of your framework-related tests for whenever you need to extend the framework.

The other thing that's important to know is the library that we'll be using. So you're about to see possibly strange syntax to you because Masonite uses as the PEP 8 coding standard which explains that methods should be underscores, but the Masonite testing suite uses the built-in `unittest` testing library to write its tests and then recommends `pytest` to actually run the tests.

The reason we use the built-in `unittest` library is because it's actually much easier to conceptually understand than `pytest` and the reason we recommend pytest to actually run the test suite is it has a much easier to use command line tool. So by combining the good parts of `unittest` with the good parts of `pytest`, we are able to make testing with Masonite perfect.

The unit test the library was created before the PEP 8 standard existed so our unit tests will be created using primarily `camelCase`. Because we didn't want developers to have to switch between standard when creating their tests, all testing methods and assertions use `camelCase`. This way you can mentally prepare yourself to use (and keep using) `camelCase`.

Creating Tests

Now that we understand what we're about to see, let's get into creating our first test case and take a look at what that looks like.

So to create your test, you'll run a simple craft command:

```
$ craft test Home
```

This will create a basic boilerplate test inside `tests/test_home.py`. We can leave it here, but let's just take that and drag that into the `unit` directory so we'll have a `tests/unit/test_home.py` file.

If we open up this file, we'll see that we have three basic parts that we'll talk about now. Here is an example of what you should see:

```
"""TestHomee Testcase."""

from masonite.testing import TestCase

class TestHome(TestCase):

    """..."""
    transactions = True
```

```
def setUp(self):
    """..."""
    super().setUp()

def setUpFactories(self):
    """..."""
    pass
```

Let's walk through the code from top to bottom.

The first line we have is just a normal import of the TestCase class. This has all the methods, custom assertions, and setup logic that we will use for creating and running our tests.

The next thing you'll see is the class name. All tests need to start with Test so that the testing library knows to run it as a test and not a normal class.

Moving on you will see a transaction = True attribute. This will let Masonite know if it should run all tests inside transactions or not. Running tests inside transactions is useful so you can run tests over and over again with the same state of your database.

Next you'll see here is a setUp method. The setUp method will run before your test gets created. So if you need to do things like modify your container and override some default behavior or some default values, you'll do so in the setup method.

Lastly you'll see a setUpFactories method. This method is similar to the setup method, but here is where you'll do things like seed your database, run any factories that you have, create users, and everything else needed at the database level to get your tests set up. For example, if you have an endpoint that needs to test that there's 50 users, it might be good to create 50 users before you run that test.

The last thing that's important to note is that all tests by default must run inside of SQLite database. The reason for this is that there's times where you accidentally can screw up your production database or even your normal development database if you're using something like MySQL or Postgres. If you want, you can disable this by setting sqlite = False on your test cases. This way you can run your tests for any database.

Our First Test

Our testing methods should all be underscore and they will begin with test_underscore. Now let's build our first test.

We will be building on to the TestHome test we created in the previous section:

For page length sake, we will only focus on our method, but make sure you attach it to our test case.

```
def test_can_visit_homepage(self):
    self.get('/').assertContains('Masonite')
```

If you are writing this test from a base installation of Masonite, then this test should work since the front page shows the Masonite splash page. If you have modified the application, then change `Masonite` to whatever text you can visually see on the home page (your /route).

Also any method that starts with `assert` is able to be chained together. So let's also check if the status is 200:

```
def test_can_visit_homepage(self):
    self.get('/').assertContains('Masonite').assertIsStatus(200)
```

Now we can run this test with `pytest`. If you don't have it installed, you can install it now:

```
$ pip install pytest
```

Now we can go right to our terminal and just run:

```
$ python -m pytest
```

The reason we use `python -m pytest` and not just `pytest` is that the former will add the current working directory to the system path. This means that our tests will be able to find things like routes, models, and anything else inside our application.

Given When Then

A good tip for trying to find out how you will structure tests is using a simple "Given .. When .. Then .. " format. For example, you might break a test case down to "**Given** I am a guest user, **When** I go to the home route, I **Then** will be redirected."

This test may be broken down like this:

```
def test_guest_will_be_redirected(self):
    # Given .. I am a guest user
    # When .. I go to the home route
    response = self.get('/home')

    # Then I will be redirected
    response.assertIsStatus(302)
```

Here is another example: "**Given** I am an authenticated user, **When** I go to the home route, **Then** I should see the home page":

```
def test_user_sees_home_page(self):
    # Given .. I am an authenticated user
    response = self.actingAs(User.find(1))

    # When .. I go to the home route
    response = self.get('/home')

    # Then .. I should get redirected
    response.assertIsStatus(302)
```

Sometimes tests are really complex so breaking them down into simple steps like this makes the tests really clear.

Test-Driven Development

I would be extremely remiss if I did not at least touch upon test-driven development. Now that we have some basics of what tests are and a background on how to create them, let's talk about test-driven development, or TDD for short. TDD is the art of writing the tests first and then writing the code second.

We can take the last test as an example. There we asserted that "**Given** .. I am an authenticated user" and "**When** .. I go to the home route." Just these two steps will fail as soon as we run our tests. So what we can do is keep running our tests until we can pass them.

In this case we need to first have users. So we might start by creating some users. The next error we'll run into is the home route. We will get an error since a home route doesn't exist.

Now that we have users and a home route, we can pass the user into the route and hit that endpoint. Once done, we can finally make our assertions. A good assertion in this case might be if the user can actually visit the home page or if they get redirected.

The benefit that TDD has over other ways of testing, like writing tests after, is that it makes testing easier. If you start with a test, your code needs to be inherently testable. If you write tests after, it may be hard to test parts of your app because you might not have been thinking of how you'll test it later.

For example, you might have some kind of logic inside your controller which executes all the time. If you don't want to run that piece of code inside your test, then you might set some kind of option on the controller or even a setter method like `withoutComplexLogicOption` on your controller **specifically** so you can get around this challenge for your tests. The method might not have any practical usage in terms of the larger domain logic, but it is a testable piece of code, and you will be able to safely refactor.

I personally like test-driven development over other options and use it when building Masonite very frequently. In fact, if someone opens a pull request for a feature or issue, instead of telling them how to fix a use case they may have missed, I will write them a quick test and tell them to make sure the test passes before the pull request can merge in. This allows them to plug that test into their code and keep working until the code works. Very powerful stuff.

Factories

Factories are really useful pieces of code that allows you to quickly generate mock data on the fly. Whether you simply just want a mock user or you have a complex **When** clause you need to fulfill, factories are the way to get the data into your database before running your tests.

Creating Factories

Factories are all stored inside the `config/factories.py` file. This requires a function to return a, usually random, set of data which can be ran once or several times to mock data we can use for later. For example, Masonite comes with a default factory for creating users. We are able to use these factories in seeds and tests.

In order to create a factory, you must register the factory to a model. We will be using our Subscription model we made a few chapters back in the databases chapter.

We can easily create a factory by creating a new function inside the config/ factories.py and return a simple dictionary of column values. The format of the factory will look something like this:

```
from app.Subscription import Subscription
# ...

def subscription_factory(faker):
    return {
      'url': faker.uri(),
      'title': faker.sentence()
    }

factory.register(Subscription, systems_factory)
```

Notice we simply imported our model and then mapped our model to our factory function. The factory function takes an instance of faker which is a popular Python library which is able to very quickly generate mock data.

Using Factories

We can now use these factories in any part of our application. We can just import the factory and the model and then use it:

```
from config.factories import factory
from app.Subscription import Subscription
# ...

systems = factory(Subscription, 50).create()
```

The systems variable now holds a collection of 50 systems. We can now do whatever we need to in our tests. In the next few sections, we will use this factory to set up our tests.

If you want to just create a single model, we can easily get a single system:

```
system = factory(Subscription).create()
```

Asserting Database Values

Most times you will be asserting that you have specific database values. Maybe you create a new user and then need to make sure that user was persisted to your database. Let's say we had a POST route to create new users. Our test may look something like this:

```
def test_create_users(self):
  self.post('/users', {
    'username': 'user123',
    'email': 'user@example.com',
    'password': 'pass123'
  })

  self.assertDatabaseHas('users.email', 'user@example.com')
```

Notice we can easily assert that the email column on the users table contains the value user@example.com.

Testing Environments

When Masonite detects that a test is being ran (because of specific environment variables that are set when tests run), it will **additionally** load a .env.testing file, if one exists. This file can contain environment variables that are different than your standard .env file.

For example, you may use a RabbitMQ driver for queue jobs during development and production but may choose instead to use the more basic async driver for testing. This way we don't need to have our queue server running just for tests.

To change your environment variables for testing, you can create a .env.testing file and put variables in it like so:

```
DEBUG=True
DB_CONNECTION=sqlite
DB_DATABASE=testing.db
# ...
```

These will override any existing environment variables of the same name.

CHAPTER 13

Deploying Masonite

There are many services that make the life cycle of an application extremely simple. These services include things like Heroku or Python anywhere. In this chapter, we will mainly focus on deploying your application manually, low level, and on your own from scratch by provisioning a server, installing required software, and installing and running our application. If you know how to do these low-level tasks and understand the bigger picture, then you can easily figure out how to use a point and click system like Heroku.

It's important to note that parts of this chapter require a payment method to set a server up and deploy your application.

The Request Life Cycle

Let's talk about what happens when you enter a domain name into the web browser and hit Enter. Once we do this, you should have enough background information to start fitting ourselves in this life cycle.

When you type in `masoniteproject.com` and hit Enter in your web browser (like Chrome or Firefox), the web browser will build a request. The request contains a bunch of meta information in the form of headers. At this point our request goes on a mission to convert `masoniteproject.com` into an IP address so the Internet knows how to direct that request to the server.

We can do this conversion by doing a DNS (domain name system) lookup. There is a domain system on our local computer (think your hosts file), at our internal network (think how companies block certain web sites or have certain web sites only accessible from inside the office), and then at the Internet level (think Cloudflare or Namecheap DNS).

© Christopher Pitt and Joe Mancuso 2020
C. Pitt and J. Mancuso, *The Definitive Guide to Masonite*, https://doi.org/10.1007/978-1-4842-5602-2_13

Assuming we have no special instructions at the local or internal network level, that request, which is still in search of an IP address, will go to Cloudflare. Cloudflare is a DNS provider that is pretty popular because of their generous free plan. Cloudflare gets the request, looks in their own system, and says "Ok yeah, I have a record here of `masoniteproject.com` with the IP address of `17.154.195.7`".

At this point the request now knows where to go. The Internet then routes that request to a server hosted on Vultr. The request connects to the server and then directs all web traffic to a port which is usually port 80. There is an application listening for all traffic on port 80 called NGINX. NGINX receives the request and says "Ok the current domain name is `masoniteproject.com` and I have a Python application listening to all requests to be redirected to it for this domain."

NGINX redirects that domain to another port called port 8001, or socket, but more on this later.

Now this part is important and is specific to Python applications. Before the request hits our Masonite application, yet another conversion needs to happen. We need to convert the incoming request to a Python dictionary and send the dictionary through our application.

This middleman conversion that happens is called a WSGI server. Since the conversion of the request is fairly straightforward, there have been several that have been built for Python. The most common ones include Gunicorn and uWSGI. These can also be swapped out at any time. Gunicorn is extremely easy to start, but uWSGI is easier to configure and has a lot of different options you can play with to tweak the settings.

Once the conversion from a request to a dictionary is done, it passes that dictionary into the Masonite framework and the Masonite framework calls all relevant parts of your Masonite application and returns a response in bytes. The WSGI server then converts those Python bytes into a response that NGINX will understand.

That request, which now has a response from Masonite attached to it, works its way all the way back through the entire flow but in reverse now. Eventually the request and response make it all the way back to your web browser and your web browser converts that response to what you see.

Now that we know how the entire life cycle works, we can work on what we need to do in order to fit ourselves and our new application into this life cycle.

The major things we need to do are as follows:

- Set up a web server (Digital Ocean, Vultr, etc.).

- Install special software on our web server (NGINX and other packages).

- Get our Masonite application onto our web server (git cloning).

- Run our Masonite application (so NGINX can direct the response to our application).

The Web Server

The first part is a web server. This is traditionally a physical server in some companies' warehouse, but we have come a long way in how servers work, so in reality it might actually be just an isolated piece of a physical machine. However, for the purposes of explanation, this server will be a physical server.

A web server is really just a normal computer with special software installed that can accept incoming requests and produce a response to send back to your web browser. Keep in mind this "special software" because we will explain this in more detail later.

In fact, ANY computer can be a web server. I personally used to host all my web sites from a desktop computer in my basement back before I learned how insecure it was or how close I was from an attack that could take my Internet down or expose some sensitive information. Those were my early days of programming. I had to make sure my computer was always on. I remember getting messages that my web site was down only to find that my desktop computer went to sleep or my power momentarily went out and my computer never rebooted properly.

Now there are many companies that can supply you these web servers for relatively cheaply. You could get a basic server for around $5 per month which could host several sites for you.

The biggest companies individuals choose include

- Digital Ocean

- Vultr

- Linode

A lot of business choose companies like AWS (Amazon Web Services) and Microsoft. For the purposes of this book, we will be using my personal favorite: Vultr.

It's also important to note that these web servers typically do not contain a GUI and are strictly terminal based (think the original Microsoft DOS system or using your computer only via its terminal). This is because the web server should really only be doing one thing, which is handling web traffic. Anything that is running on the web server that doesn't promote this goal is needless overhead, so when you set your server up, don't be surprised if you only see a black terminal screen.

Setting Up the Server

Let's talk about how to set the server up. We will be using Vultr for this book. If we go to Vultr.com, create an account, and go to the dashboard, we will see a screen that looks like Figure 13-1.

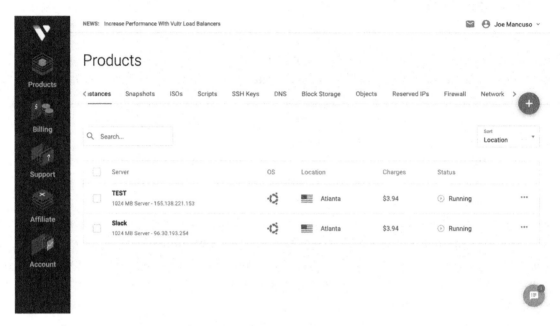

Figure 13-1. *The Vultr.com dashboard*

It's important to note that the rest of this chapter requires a payment method to set a server up and deploy your application.

If you made it in the Masonite Slack channel, you will see we have a server for that web site, and we also have a server for random testing we need to do like going through tutorials or mocking Linux issues people have.

On the top right, we will see a + icon. When we click that, we will be presented with a screen with a bunch of different options to choose from.

The Options

The first thing we need is to choose the type of server. We are currently presented with four options, as shown in Figure 13-2.

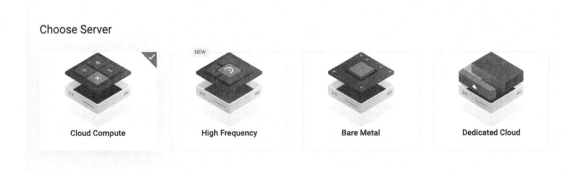

Figure 13-2. *Selecting the type of server desired*

We can choose whichever option best fits our needs, but for the most part, the first option is fine. This is a pretty standard box we can use in the cloud and fits what we need perfectly.

Next, we are presented with a list of locations on where we want the server to be, as shown in Figure 13-3. **It's important to note that you should choose the server that is closest to your audience.** The closer the server is to your audience, the faster the server response times will be.

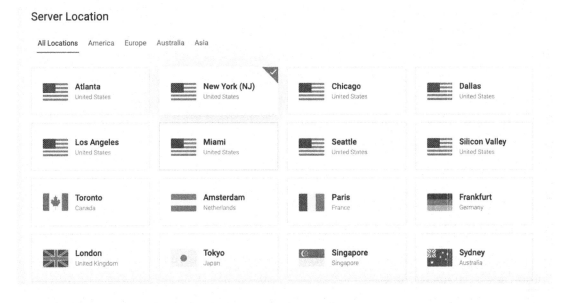

Figure 13-3. *Choosing the server location*

As illustrated in Figure 13-4, the next step is we will need to select the server type. One of the most popular options is Ubuntu.

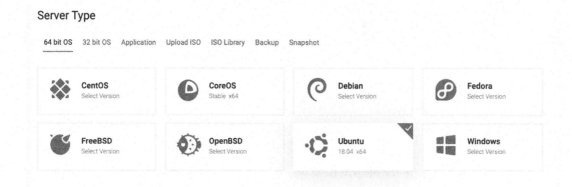

Figure 13-4. *Choosing the server type*

The last step is picking the server size. I've found that most of my Masonite apps run at around 150MB of memory, and you should have some room for a buffer since some parts of your app may need more memory than other parts, and you'll also be installing a database most likely, so you may have spikes. I recommend leaving around 20% of memory free to not slow down your applications.

So if you choose the 512MB server and leave 20% free, then you will have about 409MB of space to work with. Some of that space will be dedicated to other applications, so a 512MB server can likely run anywhere from two to three Masonite applications. This rule is not universal and is very application specific, so you should monitor your server performance before adding additional applications.

There are several options at the bottom of this page, like setting up SSH keys and startup scripts, but those can be skipped for now.

Connecting to the Server

Once the server is done provisioning (installing all the necessary operating system software), we can now connect to it and start installing all the things we need to get our Python applications running.

When you click on the new server you just built, you will see some connection credentials, as shown in Figure 13-5. On the left, you will see "IP Address," "Username," and "Password."

Location:	🇺🇸 Atlanta	CPU:	1 vCore	Label:	TEST
IP Address:	155.138.221.153	RAM:	1024 MB	Tag:	[Click here to set]
Username:	root	Storage:	25 GB SSD	OS:	Ubuntu 18.04 x64
Password:	······· 👁	Bandwidth:	0.31 GB of 1000 GB		

Figure 13-5. *Your server's connection credentials*

You will use those three settings to connect to the server and start running commands. If you are using Mac or Linux, you can use the built-in ssh command that comes in the terminal. If you are using Windows, you will need to use something like PuTTY.

I have found the majority of developers use Mac and Linux, so we will demonstrate this route to connect to the server.

First, open the terminal on your Mac or Linux machine and run this command:

```
$ ssh {username}@{host}
```

Replace username and host with the username and the IP address you see in the dashboard. Once ran, you will see another prompt asking you for your password. Go back to your dashboard and either click the eye to present your password or you can click the copy icon to copy it. Paste the password into the prompt and your terminal will then change to be the terminal of the server. You should see something like this:

```
Last login: Sun Feb 16 13:39:21 2020 from 69.119.199.3
root@{server name}:~#
```

Congratulations! You have connected to the server, and we can now start installing everything you need to get up and running. Let's move on to installing any required software.

Web Server Software

In the previous section, we said we would explain the "special software" in more detail. The web server will need some software installed on it to tell it how it should handle the web traffic that goes into it. There are two main players in web server software.

The first is **NGINX**. In my experience this is by far the most popular web server software to use. Within the last decade, it has really taken dominance in the web server world. NGINX is pretty straightforward to set up and is made to be extremely extendable and pluggable with the style of its configuration files. We will be using this option for deploying our Masonite application.

The second is **Apache**. This is a bit older standard software that people used and is still used by many companies today. It has certainly fallen out of favor for NGINX but is still a viable option. It takes a bit longer to set up than NGINX and a bit harder to configure.

The way this software works for our use case is it simply takes the incoming request and redirects it to go to a specific application on the server. So, for example, we may have a Laravel PHP application and a Python Masonite application; NGINX will direct the request to go to each one.

Web server software can also do many other things like load balancing, email server proxying, and performing communication on many other protocols, but for our purposes, it will just be redirecting a request into our application.

For the sake of this book, we will be working with NGINX.

Installing NGINX

The first thing we need to do is install NGINX. Remember that this software is responsible for taking an incoming request, routing it to get a response from the correct application, and then sending it back out to be eventually returned to your browser.

So if we test this flow, now we can see there is a disconnect. Just go to your browser and type in your IP address that you got from your Vultr dashboard. You will see an error page like the one shown in Figure 13-6.

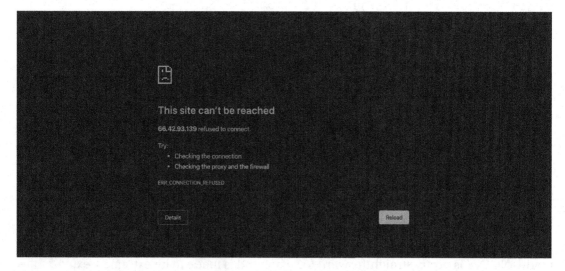

Figure 13-6. *A redirect error message*

So let's install NGINX so we can get this functionality working.

Before we install anything, we need to update our Ubuntu package directory:

```
$ apt-get update
```

Next, we can simply install NGINX. Just run this command:

```
$ apt-get install nginx
```

Let the install steps run. If you are prompted for a Yes or No question confirming if you want to install NGINX, just type Y and hit Enter.

Once installed, we can go back to our web browser and type in our IP address again. We will now see an NGINX loading page:

Welcome to nginx!

If you see this page, the nginx web server is successfully installed and working. Further configuration is required.

For online documentation and support please refer to nginx.org.
Commercial support is available at nginx.com.

Thank you for using nginx.

Remember NGINX has to redirect the request to some place to get the response, so along with NGINX installing, NGINX also has some static web pages to server to just confirm it installed properly.

NGINX needs some additional configuring, but we will get this configured when we get our application on our new server.

Setting Up Python Software

If you installed Masonite before, you likely read the documentation for installing Masonite.

The Linux packages you'll need are

- python3-dev
- python3-pip
- libssl-dev
- build-essential
- python3-venv
- git

You can install them all at the same time by using a space between each package when using the `apt-get install` command from before:

```
$ apt-get install python3-dev python3-pip libssl-dev build-essential python3-venv git
```

Once installed, you have everything you need to get Masonite up and running.

Configuring NGINX

The next step we need to do is tell NGINX where to redirect the request to. To do this, we will need to slightly configure NGINX. Luckily we just need to add a few lines of configuration.

To find out where we need to add this configuration, we need to check our main NGINX config file. We can find this location by running

```
$ nginx -t
```

This `-t` flag will test the configuration file but also conveniently output its location. We should see a result like this:

```
root@{server name}:~# nginx -t nginx: the configuration file
/etc/nginx/nginx.conf syntax is ok nginx: configuration file
/etc/nginx/nginx.conf test is successful
```

This `/etc/nginx/nginx.conf` location is where our NGINX config lives, so we can open it to find the location of where we will put our few lines of application configuration.

Let's view the contents of this file by running

```
cat/etc/nginx/nginx.conf
```

The cat command will show the contents of the file. If we scroll up a bit, we will see a section like this:

```
##
# Virtual Host Configs
##

include /etc/nginx/conf.d/*.conf;
include /etc/nginx/sites-enabled/*;
```

In addition to all the configuration settings, there are these two lines. These will simply append any configuration files in these locations. So instead of adding everything to this file and having a giant configuration file, we can add our configs to these directories and they will automatically be added here for the purposes of how NGINX reads the configurations.

So now we can go to this directory and start building what will become our application configuration file:

```
$ cd /etc/nginx/sites-enabled
$ nano example.com.conf
```

The nano command will present you with a terminal-based editor you can use to create the file. I typically will have one web application per domain name, so whatever you expect your domain name to be called, you can enter that instead of "example.com", but feel free to name this file whatever you want.

If at any time we want to close out the editor, we can do so by hitting "Ctrl+X," typing Y, and then hitting Enter.

You should now be presented with a blank editor. Let's start building our configuration file. I'll show the full file and we will go over it line by line after:

```
server {
    listen 80;
    server_name {ip address};

    location / {
        include uwsgi_params;
        uwsgi_pass unix:///srv/sockets/{example.com}.sock;
        proxy_request_buffering off;
        proxy_buffering off;
        proxy_redirect off;
    }
}
```

In order to prevent additional steps during a deployment, we will be using sockets. Sockets are simply files that both NGINX and our WSGI server will be able to stream to and from to get the necessary information they need. This way we will not be listening on a port and will not need to restart our application between deployments. This will improve downtime.

So going from top to bottom, we have what's called a "server block." This is simply a block of configurations. Remember this will essentially be included in the main NGINX configuration file, so it will need to be wrapped in a block to isolate these settings.

The next thing we see is a `port` to listen to. This will most likely always be port 80 because, by default, all web traffic will travel on port 80.

The next line is a `server_name`. If you have a domain name, you can enter that here. If not, you can simply put the server's IP address here.

Next, we have another block, but this time it is a `location` block. We want all traffic to be directed to our application, so we will put a base location of /.

Inside the block, we will put `include uwsgi_params;` This sets special headers that our WSGI server will need to build our Python dictionary to be passed into the Masonite framework.

The next is a `uwsgi_pass` line. This will stream the traffic to a socket file which our WSGI server will stream from as well. So this is the communication point between NGINX and our WSGI server. The line really starts with `unix://` and everything after that is a directory path. We set up `/srv/sockets/` to be the directory which will hold all the sockets.

Lastly, we have a few proxy settings which configure some of the behavior of the connection.

Once that is configured, we can then close out the editor by hitting "Ctrl+X," typing Y, and then hitting Enter.

Reloading NGINX

You may also have to reload NGINX so we can run another simple command:

```
$ nginx -s reload
```

Testing Everything Worked

You can make sure everything worked by now heading back to your IP address in the browser. If you put your IP address in your application config, you should now see a gateway error, as shown in Figure 13-7.

502 Bad Gateway

nginx/1.14.0 (Ubuntu)

Figure 13-7. *A Bad Gateway error message*

This is a good thing. This means that NGINX is trying to communicate correctly with our Masonite application (which is not installed properly).

Set Up Tasks

There are a few things we put into the config file that doesn't exist yet like the /srv/ sockets directory. So we can make that now:

```
$ mkdir -p /srv/sockets
```

We need to also make sure both NGINX and our application have permission to access this directory so we can run another simple command:

```
$ chmod 0777 /srv/sockets
```

Setting Up Our Application

Ok, now we can finally get to the good stuff – setting up our Masonite application.

I personally like to put everything in a /srv/sites directory to keep everything nice and clean. So let's make that directory now:

```
$ mkdir -p /srv/sites
```

Now we can git clone our repository to this directory. This example repo will be hosted on GitHub, so our link will look like this:

```
$ git clone https://github.com/username/repo.git example
$ cd example
```

Replace `username` and `repo` with the username and repo of your GitHub project. If you do not have one, you can use `masoniteframework` and `cookie-cutter` as the username and repo, respectively.

This will now put our application in a `/srv/sites/example` directory.

Running the Application

The next thing we have to do is install and run our application. This part you are already used to, and there are not many changes between development on your machine and this server. We just need to create a virtual environment again and install our Python packages:

```
$ python3 -m venv /venvs/example
$ source /venvs/example/bin/activate
$ pip install -r requirements.txt
```

Our Masonite app should be fully installed now and we can now run it.

In order to run our application, we will be using uWSGI. We can install uWSGI now and run a simple command to get us started:

```
$ pip install uwsgi $ uwsgi
--socket /srv/sockets/example.com.sock --wsgi-file wsgi.py \
    --chmod-socket=777 --pidfile /srv/sockets/example.com.pid &>
/dev/null &
```

Just make sure the location of this socket is the same as the location of the socket you put in the application configuration file. We also use a `--chmod-socket` command which will give uWSGI the correct permissions. The permission stuff is a little tricky, and without it, you will run into strange issues where it looks like the application is not running. You will continue to get 502 errors.

We have a `--wsgi-file wsgi.py` line which simply runs the `wsgi.py` file in the root of all Masonite applications. This is the entry point for Masonite applications that need to run via a WSGI server.

You will also notice a strange `&> /dev/null` & syntax at the end. This tells uwsgi to run this command in the background. This way we can exit the server or perform other server actions but still have the application running.

You will also notice we put a `--pidfile` flag. What this does is it connects a file to this instance of the application. The problem is in the future; we can kill it at any time by simply killing the PID file.

If the preceding steps did not work for any reason, you can check the error logs for NGINX. The error logs are most likely located at `/var/log/nginx/error.log` and can be checked by running

```
$ cat /var/log/nginx/error.log
```

Use the contents of the file to start debugging any issues.

If the path does not exist, you can find the path in the main nginx config file at the line that looks like

```
error_log /var/log/nginx/error.log;
```

Now finally you can go to the server for the last time in your web browser and you will now see your Masonite application running!

It's important to note here that running a server is not as simple as putting web applications on a server and running them. Maintaining a server includes things like security updates, managing deployments and file permissions, and keeping third-party services running like databases, supervisor, and a lot more. You will have to manage the uptime of your application. If anything goes wrong, you will need to SSH back into the server and debug what is wrong.

It may be wiser to go with a third-party service like Heroku to manage all of this for you. Starter plans start at a low fee of a few bucks per month.

Deployments

In the previous section, we explained how to set up a server and perform a deployment. There are two types of deployments you will use: manual deployments and automatic deployments.

Manual deployments are when you SSH back into the server, kill the previous running instance of your application, and then start up the new one.

Automatic deployments are when a service performs all these steps before you to get a new version of your application up and running. These actions could be things like when a new commit is made to your master branch or when you cut a new release.

Manual Deployments

If you want to perform a manual deployment, you will SSH back into your server, kill the PID file, update the codebase, and then rerun the uWSGI serve command.

For example, when we first started our application, we had a flag like this:

```
--pidfile /srv/sockets/example.com.pid
```

This connected the lifeline of our running application to the lifeline of this PID file. Kill the PID file and you kill the application. You can kill the PID file by running

```
uwsgi --stop /srv/sockets/example.com.pid
```

Now that the application is dead, it is no longer accessible. We can now restart the application.

1. Activate the application's virtual environment:

   ```
   source /venvs/example/bin/activate
   ```

2. Go to directory and git pull the new code changes (this depends on the branch or commit you want to deploy):

   ```
   $ cd /srv/sites/example
   $ git pull -f https://github.com/username/repo.git master
   ```

3. Install any new requirements:

   ```
   $ pip install -r requirements.txt
   ```

4. Run the `uwsgi` command to start the application described in the "Running the Application" section:

```
$ uwsgi --socket /srv/sockets/example.com.sock --wsgi-file wsgi.py \
    --chmod-socket=777 --pidfile /srv/sockets/example.com.pid &> /
    dev/null &
```

Automatic Deployments

You can use many automatic deployments if you want as well. There are many services that do this for you that are very well documented online, and it would be ill advised to try and replicate that documentation in this book, but one of my favorites is Heroku. This is a **very** easy service that is generally point and click with very few terminal commands locally to get your service up and running.

You may also check the Masonite documentation for additional links on getting other forms of automatic deployments such as performing a commit on GitHub or cutting a release which will do most of the steps in this chapter for you. Links can be found in the main online documentation.

Index

A

Active Record database pattern, 99
after method, 136
AJAX calls, 108, 109
Amazon Web Services (AWS), 187
Aptitude, 6
Asserting database values, 183
Authentication, 123
    auth-related files, 124
    LoginController, 125
    email field, 127, 128
    email verification, 132, 133
    logged out, 129
    Masonite, 134
    new user creation, 126, 127
    RegisterController, 125
    user logging, 129
auth() function, 144, 145
Auth helper, 143, 144
auth middleware, 131, 136
Automated testing, 176

B

before method, 136
bind method, 42, 45
    class *vs.* object behavior, 45, 46
    singletons, 47

Secure forms, building
    CSRF protection, 69, 71
    pages, 64
    podcasts/search.html template, 65, 66
    template filters, 68, 69
    templates conditionals, 66, 67

C

Cache-Control header, 118
--chmod-socket command, 198
Cleans request input, 106
Cloudflare, 186
Common Vulnerabilities and Exposures
    (CVE), 119
compact() function, 147
config() function, 147
Constructing middleware
    after method, 136
    before method, 136
    initializer, 135, 136
Container helper, 146
Controllers, 14–17
Cookies, 121, 122
craft auth command, 109, 130
craft command, 124, 135, 168
craft key command, 120
Cross-Origin Resource Sharing
    (CORS), 115, 116

© Christopher Pitt and Joe Mancuso 2020
C. Pitt and J. Mancuso, *The Definitive Guide to Masonite*, https://doi.org/10.1007/978-1-4842-5602-2

Printed in the United States
By Bookmasters